Betty Crocker's

RED SPOON COLLECTION™

BEST RECIPES FOR SENSATIONAL DESSERTS

PRENTICE HALL

New York London Toronto Sydney Tokyo Singapore

Prentice Hall
15 Columbus Circle
New York, New York 10023

Published simultaneously in Canada by Prentice Hall Canada Inc.

PRENTICE HALL and colophon are registered
trademarks of Simon & Schuster, Inc.

BETTY CROCKER is a registered trademark
of General Mills, Inc.

RED SPOON COLLECTION is a trademark of General Mills, Inc.

Library of Congress Cataloging-in-Publication Data

Best recipes for sensational desserts.—1st ed.
   p. cm.—(Betty Crocker's Red Spoon collection)
  Includes index.
  1. Desserts. I. Series.
TX773.B4865 1990
641.8′6—dc20   89-8404
                                     CIP

Manufactured in the United States of America

10 9 8 7 6 5 4 3 2 1

First Prentice Hall Edition

Front Cover: Frozen Mocha-Almond Dessert, (left), Strawberry Glacé Pie, (top),
and German Chocolate Cake, (right)

CONTENTS

INTRODUCTION

Sensational Desserts

What makes a dessert sensational? When it strikes the right chord for the occasion: fresh or rich, sweet or mysterious, homey or all-out fantastical. Dessert can be a reward, a treat, a gesture, a gift, a gracious moment or a glorious celebration. A simple dessert can make an impression every bit as elegant as something that takes all day to assemble, and the following pages offer more than one hundred finishing touches, from light Watermelon with Blackberries and Pear Purée (page 88) to frankly self-indulgent German Chocolate Cheesecake (page 26).

When deciding which dessert to prepare, consider what would be an appropriate finish to the meal. A heavy meal calls for a light, refreshing dessert rather than a rich substantial one. In wintertime, baked and steamed puddings served warm are great favorites. Try Chocolate Ranch Pudding (page 59), Steamed Molasses Pudding with Lemon Sauce (page 60) and Bread Pudding with Whiskey Sauce (page 65). Ice creams, ices and sorbets were invented for enjoyment in hot weather, and our selection of Frozen Desserts (page 74)

includes exotic newcomers along with all-time favorites. Chocolate lovers will want to turn immediately to Chocolate Sundae Cake (page 9), French Silk Tart (page 37), Fudge Soufflé (page 53), Chocolate Pots de Crème (page 65) and Chocolate Terrine (page 66), just a sampling of the luxurious chocolate recipes included in this collection.

When preparing dessert for a special occasion, it makes sense to think about whom you are serving. The tastes of rum, brandy, coffee and liqueurs are more appropriate for adults than for children, who prefer simpler, more familiar flavors like chocolate, vanilla and fruit. Smooth puddings and ice creams are usually a safe bet with the under-five crowd, as is fresh fruit. Anyone who is watching his or her weight will appreciate the thoughtful inclusion of a low-calorie or low-fat dessert, and here again, fresh fruit can be a boon. Ices are fat-free, of course, as are some puddings made with fruit (just be sure to serve them without whipped cream, to keep them fat-free). People who are diabetic must avoid alcohol and sugar in all its guises, including corn syrup, molasses and honey.

Serving Desserts

Have the proper serving utensils on hand when it is time to pass the dessert plates. Nothing is more vexing than making a wreck of a pretty dessert when time and effort were spent making it attractive. A dull knife will just squash a chiffon cake, frosted or not. Always use a long, serrated knife for chiffon and angel food cakes, and cut with a gentle, sawing motion. Use a sharp, thin knife to cut shortening-type cakes. Formal servers usually cut cake well and make transporting slices intact to plates easier; just be sure you're using one with the appropriate edge, whether serrated or sharp. If frosting or glaze sticks to the knife, dip the blade into a tall glass of hot water and wipe it clean with paper toweling after cutting each slice. Have a sauceboat or serving bowl and dessert ladle ready for serving a dessert sauce; ladles are preferred for chunky sauces, which can splash when poured.

Timing

Some desserts must be made well in advance of serving (refer to page 108 for an at-a-glance listing), and they are the answer to a host's or hostess's prayer. A few desserts demand to be served just as soon as they have been made, such as the Wine Custard (page 71) and Orange Dessert Omelets (page 96). Happily, many desserts are as delicious warm as they are when they have cooled, so you can serve them at your convenience. If you are entertaining, you probably don't want to be fussing in the kitchen while your guests are at the table. Whipping cream before serving the dessert may be all you wish to do at the last minute, and if that's the case, we have a wide selection from which you can choose the ideal recipe.

Be sure to turn to Red Spoon Tips (page 97) for special decorating hints and advice on baking, storing and freezing cakes and pies. You'll find a crumb pie crust guide there, too, an easy reference for those last-minute inspirations. It doesn't have to take a lot of work to make a lasting, sweet impression, and we hope that this book helps you on your way.

· 1 ·

BLUE-RIBBON CAKES

White Chocolate Cake

16 SERVINGS

2 tablespoons white vinegar
1 cup evaporated milk
2¼ cups all-purpose flour
1½ cups sugar
¾ cup shortening
1 teaspoon baking soda
1 teaspoon vanilla
½ teaspoon salt
4 eggs
4 ounces white chocolate (vanilla-flavored candy coating), melted and cooled slightly
1 cup flaked coconut
1 cup chopped pecans
Vanilla Glaze (below)

Heat oven to 350°. Grease and flour 12-cup bundt cake pan. Stir vinegar into milk; let stand until slightly thickened, about 1 minute. Beat vinegar mixture and remaining ingredients except coconut, pecans and Vanilla Glaze in 2½-quart bowl on low speed, scraping bowl constantly, 30 seconds. Beat on high speed, scraping bowl occasionally, 3 minutes. Stir in coconut and pecans. Pour into pan.

Bake until wooden pick inserted in center of cake comes out clean, 50 to 55 minutes; cool 15 minutes. Invert on wire rack or heatproof serving plate. Remove pan; cool cake completely. Prepare Vanilla Glaze; spread over top of cake, allowing some to drizzle down side. Sprinkle with chopped pecans, if desired.

VANILLA GLAZE

2 tablespoons margarine or butter
1 cup powdered sugar
½ teaspoon vanilla
3 to 4 teaspoons evaporated milk

Heat margarine in 1-quart saucepan over low heat until melted. Stir in powdered sugar, vanilla and milk until smooth and of desired consistency.

German Chocolate Cake

1/2 cup boiling water
1 bar (4 ounces) sweet cooking chocolate
2 cups sugar
1 cup margarine or butter, softened
4 egg yolks
1 teaspoon vanilla
2 1/2 cups cake flour
1 teaspoon baking soda
1 teaspoon salt
1 cup buttermilk
4 egg whites, stiffly beaten
Coconut-Pecan Frosting (below)

Heat oven to 350°. Grease 2 square pans, 8 × 8 × 2 or 9 × 9 × 2 inches, or 3 round pans, 8 or 9 × 1 1/2 inches. Line bottoms of pans with waxed paper. Pour boiling water on chocolate, stirring until melted; cool.

Mix sugar and margarine in 3-quart bowl until light and fluffy. Beat in egg yolks, one at a time. Beat in chocolate and vanilla on low speed. Combine flour, baking soda and salt and add alternately with buttermilk, beating after each addition until batter is smooth. Fold in egg whites. Pour into pans.

Bake until wooden pick inserted in center comes out clean, 8-inch squares 45 to 50 minutes, 9-inch squares 40 to 45 minutes, 8-inch rounds 35 to 40 minutes, 9-inch rounds 30 to 35 minutes; cool. Fill layers and frost top of cake with Coconut-Pecan Frosting.

COCONUT-PECAN FROSTING

1 cup sugar
1/2 cup margarine or butter
1 cup evaporated milk
1 teaspoon vanilla
3 egg yolks
1 1/3 cups flaked coconut
1 cup chopped pecans

Mix sugar, margarine, milk, vanilla and egg yolks in saucepan. Cook over medium heat, stirring occasionally, until thick, about 12 minutes. Stir in coconut and pecans. Beat until of spreading consistency.

Chocolate Sundae Cake

2 1/3 cups all-purpose flour
1 1/2 cups sugar
1 teaspoon baking soda
1 teaspoon salt
1/2 teaspoon baking powder
1/2 cup shortening
1/2 cup water
3/4 cup buttermilk
1/2 cup chocolate syrup
1 teaspoon vanilla
2 eggs
1/2 cup chocolate syrup
Chocolate Sundae Filling (below)
1 tablespoon chocolate syrup

Heat oven to 350°. Grease and flour rectangular pan, 13 × 9 × 2 inches, 12-cup bundt cake pan, 2 round pans, 9 × 1 1/2 inches, or 3 round pans, 8 × 1 1/2 inches.

Beat all ingredients except 1/2 cup chocolate syrup, the Chocolate Sundae Filling and 1 tablespoon chocolate syrup in large mixer bowl on low speed, scraping bowl constantly, 30 seconds. Beat on medium speed, scraping bowl occasionally, 3 minutes. Reserve 1/2 cup of the batter; pour remaining batter into pan(s). Mix the remaining 1/2 cup chocolate syrup into reserved batter. Marble half the mixture into batter in each pan.

Bake until wooden pick inserted in center comes out clean, rectangular cake 40 minutes, bundt cake 50 to 55 minutes, 9-inch layers 35 minutes, 8-inch layers 25 minutes. Cool layers or bundt cake 10 minutes; remove from pan(s). Cool completely. Frost rectangular cake or fill and frost layers with Chocolate Sundae Filling and drizzle 1 tablespoon chocolate syrup over top. Or top slices of bundt cake with Chocolate Sundae Filling and drizzle with chocolate syrup. Refrigerate any remaining cake.

CHOCOLATE SUNDAE FILLING

1 cup chilled whipping cream
1/4 cup chocolate syrup

Beat whipping cream and chocolate syrup in chilled medium bowl until stiff.

Following pages: French Silk Filbert Cake, left (page 12), and German Chocolate Cake, right

French Silk Filbert Cake

White Nut Cake (below)
French Silk Frosting (page 13)
12 whole filberts
1 cup finely chopped filberts

Bake White Nut Cake as directed. Reserve ½ cup French Silk Frosting for decorating; fill layers and frost cake with remaining frosting. Mark servings on frosting with serrated knife.

Place reserved frosting in decorating bag with star tip #18. Pipe three-petaled lily onto each serving. Place a whole filbert on each lily. Press chopped filberts into frosting around side.

WHITE NUT CAKE

6 egg whites
¼ cup sugar
2⅔ cups all-purpose flour
1½ cups finely chopped filberts
1¼ cups sugar
½ cup margarine or butter, softened
½ cup shortening
4 teaspoons baking powder
1 teaspoon salt
1 cup milk

Heat oven to 350°. Grease and flour 3 round pans, 8 × 1½ inches. Beat egg whites in large bowl until foamy. Beat in ¼ cup sugar, 1 tablespoon at a time; continue beating until mixture is stiff and glossy. Do not underbeat.

Beat flour, filberts, 1¼ cups sugar, the margarine, shortening, baking powder and salt in another large bowl on medium speed, scraping bowl constantly, until blended, about 30 seconds. Beat in milk on medium speed, scraping bowl occasionally, 2 minutes; fold into egg whites. Pour into pans.

Bake until wooden pick inserted in center comes out clean, 35 to 40 minutes. (Refrigerate 1 layer while 2 are baking.) Cool 10 minutes; remove from pans. Cool completely.

FRENCH SILK FROSTING

4 cups powdered sugar
1 cup margarine or butter, softened
3 ounces unsweetened chocolate, melted
   and cooled
1½ teaspoons vanilla
3 tablespoons milk

Beat all ingredients on medium speed until frosting is smooth and of spreading consistency. If necessary, stir in additional milk, 1 teaspoon at a time.

FRENCH SILK PECAN CAKE: Substitute finely chopped pecans for finely chopped filberts. Substitute whole pecans for whole filberts.

Lemon-glazed Cake

16 SERVINGS

1½ cups sugar
½ cup margarine or butter, softened
3 eggs
2½ cups all-purpose flour
1 teaspoon baking soda
½ teaspoon salt
1 cup buttermilk
¼ cup poppy seed
2 tablespoons grated lemon peel
2 tablespoons lemon juice
Lemon Glaze (below)

Heat oven to 325°. Grease and flour 12-cup bundt cake pan or tube pan, 10 × 4 inches. Beat sugar and margarine in large bowl on medium speed until light and fluffy. Beat in eggs, one at a time.

Mix flour, baking soda and salt; beat into sugar mixture alternately with buttermilk until well blended. Stir in poppy seed, lemon peel and lemon juice. Spread in pan.

Bake until wooden pick inserted in center comes out clean, 50 to 55 minutes. Immediately poke holes in top of cake with long-tined fork; pour about ⅔ of the Lemon Glaze over top. Cool 20 minutes. Invert on heatproof serving plate; remove pan. Spread with remaining glaze.

LEMON GLAZE

2 cups powdered sugar
¼ cup margarine or butter, melted
2 tablespoons grated lemon peel
¼ cup lemon juice

Mix all ingredients.

Toasted Almond Pound Cake

2¾ cups sugar
1¼ cups margarine or butter
5 eggs
3 cups all-purpose flour
2 teaspoons ground cinnamon
1 teaspoon baking powder
¼ teaspoon salt
1 cup evaporated milk
1½ cups chopped blanched almonds, toasted
Cinnamon-Chocolate Sauce (below)
Whipped cream

Heat oven to 350°. Grease and flour 12-cup bundt cake pan or tube pan, 10 × 4 inches. Beat sugar, margarine and eggs in large bowl on low speed, scraping bowl constantly, 30 seconds. Beat batter on high speed, scraping bowl occasionally, 5 minutes.

Beat in flour, cinnamon, baking powder and salt alternately with milk, on low speed. Fold in almonds. Spread in pan.

Bake until wooden pick inserted in center comes out clean, 70 to 80 minutes. Cool 20 minutes. Invert on heatproof serving plate; remove pan. Serve with Cinnamon-Chocolate Sauce and whipped cream.

CINNAMON-CHOCOLATE SAUCE

1 cup whipping cream
½ cup sugar
3 ounces unsweetened chocolate
1 tablespoon margarine or butter
1 teaspoon ground cinnamon

Heat whipping cream, sugar and chocolate to boiling over medium heat, stirring constantly. Boil and stir until chocolate is well blended, about 30 seconds. Remove from heat; stir in margarine and cinnamon.

Apricot-glazed Pound Cake

Apricot Brandy Pound Cake (page 15)
½ cup apricot preserves
1 tablespoon apricot brandy or apricot nectar
1 can (about 8¾ ounces) apricot halves, drained
Mint leaves
1 cup dairy sour cream
¼ cup packed brown sugar

Bake Apricot Brandy Pound Cake as directed. Heat apricot preserves until melted; remove from heat. Cut up any large pieces of fruit. Stir in apricot brandy. Spread warm apricot glaze over cake. Garnish with apricot halves and mint leaves. Mix sour cream and brown sugar. Serve sweetened sour cream and any remaining apricot halves with cake.

APRICOT BRANDY POUND CAKE

3 cups all-purpose flour
3 cups sugar
1 cup margarine or butter, softened
1 cup dairy sour cream
1/2 cup apricot brandy or apricot nectar
1/2 teaspoon salt
1/4 teaspoon baking soda
1 teaspoon orange extract
1 teaspoon lemon extract
1 teaspoon almond extract
6 eggs

Heat oven to 325°. Grease and flour 12-cup bundt cake pan or tube pan, 10 × 4 inches. Beat all ingredients in large bowl on medium speed, scraping bowl constantly, until blended, about 30 seconds. Beat on high speed, scraping bowl occasionally, 2 minutes. Pour batter into pan.

Bake until wooden pick inserted in center comes out clean, 70 to 80 minutes. Cool 20 minutes; remove from pan. Cool cake completely.

Apple Cake

16 SERVINGS

1/3 cup boiling water
2 cups chopped pared apples (about 2 medium)
1 cup all-purpose flour
1 cup whole wheat flour
1 1/4 cups sugar
1/2 cup vegetable oil
1 1/4 teaspoons baking soda
1 teaspoon ground cinnamon
1 teaspoon vanilla
1/2 teaspoon salt
1/2 teaspoon ground cloves
3 eggs
Nut Topping (below)

Heat oven to 350°. Grease and flour rectangular pan, 13 × 9 × 2 inches. Pour water over apples in 3-quart bowl. Add remaining ingredients except Nut Topping. Blend on low speed, scraping bowl constantly, 1 minute. Beat on medium speed, scraping bowl occasionally, 2 minutes. Pour batter into pan; sprinkle with Nut Topping. Bake until wooden pick inserted in center comes out clean, 40 to 45 minutes.

NUT TOPPING

1/2 cup chopped nuts
2 tablespoons packed brown sugar

Mix nuts and brown sugar.

RHUBARB CAKE: Substitute 2 cups cut-up rhubarb for the apples.

Strawberries and Cream Cake

Whipped Cream Cake (below)
Whipped Cream Cheese Frosting (below)
1 pint strawberries, sliced

Bake Whipped Cream Cake as directed. Spread 1 layer with ½ cup of the Whipped Cream Cheese Frosting; top with layer of sliced strawberries. Place remaining cake layer on top. Spread thin layer of frosting on side of cake.

Place remaining frosting in decorating bag with large open star tip #4B. Pipe vertical rows on side of cake. Pipe shell border around top edge of cake. Arrange sliced strawberries on top of cake. Refrigerate remaining cake.

WHIPPED CREAM CAKE

2 cups all-purpose flour or 2¼ cups cake
  flour
1½ cups sugar
2 teaspoons baking powder
½ teaspoon salt
1½ cups chilled whipping cream
3 eggs
1½ teaspoons vanilla

Heat oven to 350°. Grease and flour 2 round pans, 8 or 9 × 1½ inches. Mix flour, sugar, baking powder and salt. Beat whipping cream in chilled medium bowl until stiff. Beat eggs in small bowl until very thick and lemon colored, about 5 minutes. Fold eggs and vanilla into whipped cream. Add flour mixture, about ½ cup at a time, folding gently after each addition until blended. Pour into pans.

Bake until wooden pick inserted in center comes out clean, 30 to 35 minutes. Cool 10 minutes; remove from pans. Cool completely.

WHIPPED CREAM CHEESE FROSTING

1 package (3 ounces) cream cheese,
  softened
1 tablespoon milk
2 cups chilled whipping cream
⅔ cup powdered sugar

Beat cream cheese and milk in chilled large bowl on low speed until smooth; beat in whipping cream and powdered sugar. Beat on high speed, scraping bowl occasionally, until stiff peaks form.

Brown Sugar Chiffon Cake
with Chocolate-Almond Filling

Brown Sugar Chiffon Cake (below)
Chocolate-Almond Filling (below)
1½ cups chilled whipping cream
⅓ cup powdered sugar
2 to 3 tablespoons almond-flavored
liqueur

Bake Brown Sugar Chiffon Cake as directed. Remove cake from pan. Split cake to make 4 layers. Fill each layer with 1 cup Chocolate-Almond Filling. Beat whipping cream and powdered sugar in chilled medium bowl until stiff; fold in liqueur. Frost cake with whipped cream mixture. Refrigerate any remaining cake.

BROWN SUGAR CHIFFON CAKE

2 cups all-purpose flour
¾ cup granulated sugar
¾ cup packed brown sugar
3 teaspoons baking powder
1 teaspoon salt
¾ cup cold water
½ cup vegetable oil
2 teaspoons vanilla
7 egg yolks
1 cup egg whites (about 8)
½ teaspoon cream of tartar

Heat oven to 325°. Mix flour, sugars, baking powder and salt. Beat in water, oil, vanilla and egg yolks with spoon until smooth. Beat egg whites and cream of tartar in large bowl on medium speed until stiff peaks form. Pour egg yolk mixture gradually over beaten egg whites, folding with rubber spatula just until blended. Pour into ungreased tube pan, 10 × 4 inches.

Bake until top springs back when touched lightly, about 1¼ hours. Invert on heatproof funnel; let hang until cake is cold.

CHOCOLATE-ALMOND FILLING

⅓ cup sugar
3 tablespoons cornstarch
¼ teaspoon salt
2 cups milk
2 ounces unsweetened chocolate, cut up
2 egg yolks, slightly beaten
2 tablespoons margarine or butter
2 tablespoons almond-flavored liqueur
2 teaspoons vanilla

Mix sugar, cornstarch and salt in saucepan. Stir in milk gradually; add chocolate. Cook over medium heat, stirring constantly, until chocolate is melted. Stir at least half of the hot mixture gradually into egg yolks. Blend into hot mixture in saucepan. Heat to boiling, stirring constantly. Boil and stir 2 minutes. Stir in margarine, liqueur and vanilla. Cover surface of pudding with plastic wrap; cool.

Raspberry Jam Cake

1 cup margarine or butter, softened
1/2 cup granulated sugar
1/2 cup packed brown sugar
4 eggs
1 jar (10 ounces) red raspberry preserves
   (about 1 cup)
3 1/4 cups all-purpose flour
1 teaspoon baking powder
1 teaspoon baking soda
1 teaspoon ground nutmeg
1 teaspoon ground cinnamon
1/2 teaspoon salt
1/4 teaspoon ground cloves
1 cup buttermilk
1 cup chopped pecans
Caramel Frosting (below)

Heat oven to 350°. Grease and flour tube pan, 10 × 4 inches. Beat margarine and sugars in 3-quart bowl on medium speed, scraping bowl constantly, until blended. Beat on high speed 1 minute. Beat in eggs and preserves until well blended. (Mixture will appear curdled.) Combine flour, baking powder, baking soda, nutmeg, cinnamon, salt and cloves and add alternately with buttermilk, beginning and ending with flour mixture, until well blended. Stir in pecans. Pour into pan.

Bake until wooden pick inserted in center comes out clean and top springs back when touched lightly, 70 to 75 minutes. Cool 10 minutes; remove from pan. Cool completely. Frost with Caramel Frosting.

CARAMEL FROSTING

1/2 cup margarine or butter
1 cup packed brown sugar
1/4 cup milk
2 cups powdered sugar

Heat margarine in 2-quart saucepan until melted. Stir in brown sugar. Heat to boiling, stirring constantly. Boil and stir over low heat 2 minutes; stir in milk. Heat to boiling; remove from heat. Cool to lukewarm. Gradually stir in powdered sugar; beat until smooth and of spreading consistency. If frosting becomes too stiff, stir in milk, 1 teaspoon at a time.

Zucchini Cake

1/3 cup boiling water
2 cups finely chopped zucchini (about
    3 medium)
2 cups all-purpose flour
1 1/4 cups sugar
1/2 cup vegetable oil
1 1/4 teaspoons baking soda
1 teaspoon salt
1 teaspoon ground cinnamon
1 teaspoon ground cloves
1 teaspoon ground nutmeg
1 teaspoon vanilla
3 eggs
1 cup chopped nuts
Cream Cheese Frosting (below)

CREAM CHEESE FROSTING

1 package (3 ounces) cream cheese,
    softened
1 tablespoon milk
1 teaspoon vanilla
2 1/2 cups powdered sugar

Pour boiling water over zucchini. Grease and flour rectangular pa[...] inches.

Heat oven to 350°. Beat zucchini mixture and remaining ingredients, except Cream Cheese Frosting, on medium speed, scraping bowl constantly, until blended, about 1 minute. Beat on medium speed, scraping bowl occasionally, 2 minutes. Pour into pan.

Bake until wooden pick inserted in center comes out clean, 45 to 50 minutes. Cool 10 minutes; remove from pan, if desired. Cool completely. Frost cake with Cream Cheese Frosting.

Mix cream cheese, milk and vanilla. Gradually stir in powdered sugar until smooth and of spreading consistency. If necessary, stir in additional milk, 1/2 teaspoon at a time.

Following pages: Raspberry Jam Cake

Carrot Cake

2 cups all-purpose flour
2 cups finely shredded carrots
1¼ cups sugar
½ cup vegetable oil
⅓ cup water
1¼ teaspoon baking soda
1 teaspoons salt
1 teaspoon ground cinnamon
1 teaspoon ground cloves
1 teaspoon ground nutmeg
1 teaspoon vanilla
3 eggs
1 cup chopped nuts
Cream Cheese Frosting (page 19)

Heat oven to 350°. Grease and flour 2 round pans, 8 or 9 × 1½ inches. Beat all ingredients, except Cream Cheese Frosting, in large bowl on medium speed, scraping bowl constantly, until blended, about 1 minute. Beat on medium speed, scraping bowl occasionally, 2 minutes. Pour into pans.

Bake until wooden pick inserted in center comes out clean, 35 to 40 minutes. Cool 10 minutes; remove from pans. Cool completely. Fill layers and frost top of cake with Cream Cheese Frosting.

Marbled Cheesecake

1¼ cups chocolate wafer crumbs (about 20 wafers)
2 tablespoons sugar
3 tablespoons margarine or butter, melted
1 package (6 ounces) semisweet chocolate chips
2 packages (8 ounces each) plus 1 package (3 ounces) cream cheese, softened
¼ teaspoon vanilla
1 cup sugar
3 eggs

Mix wafer crumbs, 2 tablespoons sugar and the margarine. Press in bottom of springform pan, 9 × 3 inches. Heat oven to 300°. Heat chocolate chips over low heat, stirring occasionally, until melted; cool slightly. Beat cream cheese and vanilla in 3-quart bowl until smooth. Add 1 cup sugar gradually, beating until fluffy. Beat in eggs, 1 at a time. Divide batter into halves. Stir chocolate into 1 half. Spoon batters alternately into pan. Cut through batters with knife or spatula several times for marbled effect.

Bake until center is firm, 55 to 65 minutes; cool to room temperature. Refrigerate at least 3 hours but no longer than 10 days. Loosen edge of cheesecake before removing side of pan. Refrigerate any remaining cheesecake.

Lindy's Cheesecake

1 cup all-purpose flour
1/2 cup margarine or butter, softened
1/4 cup sugar
1 tablespoon grated lemon peel
1 egg yolk
5 packages (8 ounces each) cream cheese,
    softened
1 3/4 cups sugar
3 tablespoons all-purpose flour
1 tablespoon grated orange peel
1 tablespoon grated lemon peel
1/4 teaspoon salt
5 eggs
2 egg yolks
1/4 cup whipping cream
3/4 cup chilled whipping cream

Heat oven to 400°. Lightly grease springform pan, 9 × 3 inches; remove bottom. Mix 1 cup flour, the margarine, 1/4 cup sugar, 1 tablespoon lemon peel and 1 egg yolk with hands. Press 1/3 of the mixture evenly on bottom of pan; place on cookie sheet. Bake until golden, 8 to 10 minutes; cool.

Assemble bottom and side of pan; secure side. Press remaining mixture evenly all the way up side of pan.

Heat oven to 475°. Beat cream cheese, 1 3/4 cups sugar, 3 tablespoons flour, the orange peel, 1 tablespoon lemon peel, the salt and 2 of the eggs in large bowl until smooth. Continue beating, adding remaining eggs and 2 egg yolks, 1 at a time. Beat in 1/4 cup whipping cream on low speed. Pour into pan. Bake 15 minutes.

Reduce oven temperature to 200°. Bake 1 hour. Turn off oven; leave cheesecake in oven 15 minutes. Cover and refrigerate at least 12 hours but no longer than 48 hours.

Loosen cheesecake from side of pan; remove side of pan. Beat 3/4 cup whipping cream in chilled small bowl until stiff. Spread whipped cream over top of cheesecake; decorate with toasted slivered almonds, if desired. Refrigerate any remaining cheesecake immediately.

Following pages: Marbled Cheesecake

German Chocolate Cheesecake

1¼ cups chocolate wafer or graham cracker crumbs (about 18 wafers or 16 cracker squares)
2 tablespoons sugar
3 tablespoons margarine or butter, melted
2 packages (8 ounces each) plus 1 package (3 ounces) cream cheese, softened
1 cup sugar
¼ cup cocoa
2 teaspoons vanilla
3 eggs
Coconut-Pecan Topping (below)

Heat oven to 350°. Mix crumbs and 2 tablespoons sugar; mix in margarine thoroughly. Press crumb mixture evenly on bottom of ungreased springform pan, 9 × 3 inches. Bake 10 minutes; cool.

Reduce oven temperature to 300°. Beat cream cheese in 3-quart bowl. Gradually beat in 1 cup sugar and the cocoa until fluffy; add vanilla. Beat in eggs, 1 at a time. Pour over crumb mixture. Bake until center is firm, about 1 hour. Cover and refrigerate at least 3 hours but no longer than 48 hours.

Prepare Coconut-Pecan Topping; spread over cheesecake. Loosen cheesecake from side of pan; remove side of pan. Refrigerate any remaining cheesecake immediately.

COCONUT-PECAN TOPPING

⅓ cup evaporated milk
2 tablespoons margarine or butter
2 tablespoons packed brown sugar
2 egg yolks or 1 egg
½ cup chopped pecans
½ cup flaked coconut
½ teaspoon vanilla

Cook milk, margarine, brown sugar and egg yolks in 1-quart saucepan over low heat, stirring constantly, until thickened; remove from heat. Stir in remaining ingredients; cool.

Pumpkin Cheesecake

1¼ *cups gingersnap cookie crumbs (about*
   20 two-inch cookies)
¼ *cup margarine or butter, melted*
3 *packages (8 ounces each) cream cheese,*
   softened
1 *cup sugar*
1 *teaspoon ground cinnamon*
1 *teaspoon ground ginger*
½ *teaspoon ground cloves*
1 *can (16 ounces) pumpkin*
4 *eggs*
2 *tablespoons sugar*
12 *walnut halves*
¾ *cup chilled whipping cream*

Heat oven to 350°. Mix cookie crumbs and margarine. Press evenly on bottom of ungreased springform pan, 9 × 3 inches. Bake 10 minutes; cool.

Reduce oven temperature to 300°. Beat cream cheese, 1 cup sugar, the cinnamon, ginger and cloves in 4-quart bowl on medium speed until smooth and fluffy. Add pumpkin. Beat in eggs, 1 at a time, on low speed. Pour over crumb mixture. Bake until center is firm, about 1¼ hours. Cover and refrigerate at least 3 hours but no longer than 48 hours.

Cook and stir 2 tablespoons sugar and the walnuts over medium heat until sugar is melted and nuts are coated. Immediately spread on dinner plate or aluminum foil; cool completely. Carefully break nuts apart to separate, if necessary. Cover tightly and store at room temperature up to 3 days.

Loosen cheesecake from side of pan; remove side of pan. Beat whipping cream in chilled small bowl until stiff. Spread whipped cream over top of cheesecake; arrange walnuts on top. Refrigerate any remaining cheesecake immediately.

· 2 ·

PRIZE-WINNING PIES AND COBBLERS

Pastry: One-Crust Pie

8- OR 9-INCH

*⅓ cup plus 1 tablespoon shortening or
    ⅓ cup lard
1 cup all-purpose flour
½ teaspoon salt
2 to 3 tablespoons cold water*

10-INCH

*½ cup shortening or ¼ cup plus
    3 tablespoons lard
1⅓ cups all-purpose flour
½ teaspoon salt
3 to 4 tablespoons cold water*

Pastry: Two-Crust Pie

8- OR 9-INCH

*⅔ cup plus 2 tablespoons shortening or
    ⅔ cup lard
2 cups all-purpose flour
1 teaspoon salt
4 to 5 tablespoons cold water*

Cut shortening into flour and salt until particles are size of small peas. Sprinkle in water, 1 tablespoon at a time, tossing with fork until all flour is moistened and pastry almost cleans side of bowl (1 to 2 teaspoons water can be added if necessary).

Gather pastry into a ball; shape into flattened round on lightly floured cloth-covered board. (For Two-Crust Pie, divide pastry into halves and shape into 2 rounds.) Roll pastry 2 inches larger than inverted pie plate with floured cloth-covered rolling pin. Fold pastry into fourths; unfold and ease into plate, pressing firmly against bottom and side.

For the One-Crust Pie, trim overhanging edge of pastry 1 inch from rim of plate. Fold and roll pastry under, even with plate; flute. Fill and bake as directed in recipe.

For Baked Pie Shell, heat oven to 475°. Prick bottom and side thoroughly with fork. Bake until light brown, 8 to 10 minutes; cool.

10-INCH

1 cup shortening or ¾ cup plus
  2 tablespoons lard
2⅔ cups all-purpose flour
1 teaspoon salt
7 to 8 tablespoons cold water

For the Two-Crust Pie, turn desired filling into pastry-lined pie plate. Trim overhanging edge of pastry ½ inch from rim of plate. Roll other round of pastry. Fold into fourths; cut slits so steam can escape. Place over filling and unfold. Trim overhanging edge of pastry 1 inch from rim of plate. Fold and roll top edge of pastry under lower edge, pressing on rim to seal; flute.

FLUTED PASTRY EDGES: Cover edge with 2- to 3-inch strip of aluminum foil to prevent excessive browning; remove foil during last 15 minutes of baking. Bake as directed in recipe.

Applescotch Pie

8 SERVINGS

5 cups thinly sliced pared tart apples
  (about 5 medium)
1 cup packed brown sugar
¼ cup water
1 tablespoon lemon juice
¼ cup all-purpose flour
2 tablespoons granulated sugar
¾ teaspoon salt
1 teaspoon vanilla
3 tablespoons margarine or butter
Pastry for 9-inch Two-Crust Pie
  (page 28)

Mix apples, brown sugar, water and lemon juice in 2-quart saucepan. Heat to boiling; reduce heat. Cover and simmer just until apples are tender, 7 to 8 minutes. Mix flour, granulated sugar and salt; stir into apple mixture. Cook, stirring constantly, until mixture thickens and boils. Boil and stir 1 minute; remove from heat. Stir in vanilla and margarine; cool.

Heat oven to 425°. Prepare pastry. Turn apple mixture into pastry-lined pie plate. Cover with top crust that has slits cut in it; seal and flute. Cover edge with 2- to 3-inch strip of aluminum foil to prevent excessive browning; remove foil during last 15 minutes of baking. Bake until crust is golden brown, 40 to 45 minutes.

Apple Deep-Dish Pie

12 SERVINGS

Pastry for 9-inch One-Crust Pie (page 28)
1½ cups sugar
½ cup all-purpose flour
1 teaspoon ground nutmeg
1 teaspoon ground cinnamon
¼ teaspoon salt
12 cups thinly sliced pared tart apples (about 11 medium)
2 tablespoons margarine or butter

Heat oven to 425°. Prepare pastry as directed except roll into 10-inch square. Fold pastry into halves; cut slits near center of pastry so steam can escape.

Mix sugar, flour, nutmeg, cinnamon and salt. Stir in apples. Turn into ungreased square pan, 9 × 9 × 2 inches. Dot with margarine. Cover with crust; fold edges under just inside edges of pan. Bake until juice begins to bubble through slits in crust, about 1 hour. Serve slightly warm.

Rhubarb-Strawberry Pie

8 SERVINGS

Pastry for 9-inch Two-Crust Pie (page 28)
1⅓ cups sugar
⅓ cup all-purpose flour
½ teaspoon grated orange peel, if desired
2 cups cut-up rhubarb (½-inch pieces)
2 cups sliced strawberries
2 tablespoons margarine or butter

Heat oven to 425°. Prepare pastry. Mix sugar, flour and orange peel. Toss rhubarb and strawberries together. Turn half of the rhubarb mixture into pastry-lined pie plate; sprinkle with half of the sugar mixture. Repeat with remaining rhubarb and sugar mixtures. Dot with margarine. Cover with top crust that has slits cut in it; seal and flute. Sprinkle with sugar, if desired. Cover edge with 2- to 3-inch strip of aluminum foil to prevent excessive browning; remove foil during last 15 minutes of baking.

Bake until crust is brown and juice begins to bubble through slits in crust, 40 to 50 minutes.

RHUBARB-BLUEBERRY PIE: Substitute fresh or frozen (thawed) blueberries for the strawberries.

Strawberry Glacé Pie

8 SERVINGS

9-inch Baked Pie Shell (page 28)
6 cups strawberries (about 1½ quarts)
1 cup sugar
3 tablespoons cornstarch
½ cup water
1 package (3 ounces) cream cheese,
  softened

Bake pie shell. Mash enough strawberries to measure 1 cup. Mix sugar and cornstarch in 2-quart saucepan. Stir in water and mashed strawberries gradually. Cook over medium heat, stirring constantly, until mixture thickens and boils. Boil and stir 1 minute; cool.

Beat cream cheese until smooth; spread on bottom of pie shell. Fill shell with whole strawberries; pour cooked strawberry mixture over top. Refrigerate until set, at least 3 hours.

PEACH GLACÉ PIE: Substitute 5 cups sliced peaches (7 medium) for the strawberries. To prevent discoloration, use an ascorbic acid mixture as directed on package.

Blueberry Grenadine Pie

6 SERVINGS

Pastry for 9-inch One-Crust Pie (page
  28)
2 cups fresh blueberries
½ cup sugar
1 tablespoon plus 2 teaspoons cornstarch
¼ teaspoon salt
¼ teaspoon ground cinnamon
¾ cup water
¼ cup grenadine syrup
2 teaspoons lemon juice
½ cup chilled whipping cream
1 tablespoon sugar

Prepare pastry as directed except stir in ¼ cup cornmeal with the flour. Continue as directed for Baked Pie Shell (page 28). Place blueberries in pie shell.

Mix ½ cup sugar, the cornstarch, salt and cinnamon in saucepan. Stir in water. Heat to boiling, stirring constantly. Boil and stir 1 minute. Stir in grenadine syrup and lemon juice. Pour over blueberries. Refrigerate until chilled.

Beat whipping cream and 1 tablespoon sugar in chilled small bowl until stiff. Cut pie into wedges; top with whipped cream.

Following pages: Coconut Cream Pie, left (page 35), and Rhubarb-Strawberry Pie, right

Lemon Meringue Pie

9-inch Baked Pie Shell (page 28)
1½ cups sugar
⅓ cup plus 1 tablespoon cornstarch
1½ cups water
3 egg yolks, slightly beaten
3 tablespoons margarine or butter
2 teaspoons grated lemon peel
½ cup lemon juice
2 drops yellow food color, if desired
Meringue for 9-Inch Pie (below)

Bake pie shell. Heat oven to 400°. Mix sugar and cornstarch in 1½-quart saucepan. Gradually stir in water. Cook over medium heat, stirring constantly, until mixture thickens and boils. Boil and stir 1 minute. Gradually stir at least half of the hot mixture into egg yolks. Stir into hot mixture in saucepan. Boil and stir 1 minute; remove from heat. Stir in margarine, lemon peel, lemon juice and food color. Pour into pie shell.

Prepare meringue; spoon onto hot pie filling. Spread over filling, carefully sealing meringue to edge of crust to prevent shrinking or weeping.

Bake until delicate brown, 8 to 12 minutes. Cool pie away from draft. Refrigerate any remaining pie immediately.

MERINGUE FOR 9-INCH PIE

3 egg whites
¼ teaspoon cream of tartar
6 tablespoons sugar
½ teaspoon vanilla

Beat egg whites and cream of tartar in 2½-quart bowl until foamy. Beat in sugar, 1 tablespoon at a time; continue beating until stiff and glossy. Do not underbeat. Beat in vanilla.

BROWN SUGAR MERINGUE: Substitute packed brown sugar for the granulated sugar.

Sour Cream–Raisin Meringue Pie

9-inch Baked Pie Shell (page 28)
1 tablespoon plus 1½ teaspoons cornstarch
1 cup plus 2 tablespoons sugar
¼ teaspoon salt
¾ teaspoon ground nutmeg
1½ cups dairy sour cream
3 egg yolks
1½ cups raisins
1 tablespoon lemon juice

Bake pie shell. Reduce oven temperature to 400°. Mix cornstarch, sugar, salt and nutmeg in 2-quart saucepan. Stir in sour cream. Stir in egg yolks, raisins and lemon juice. Cook over medium heat, stirring constantly, until mixture thickens and boils. Boil and stir 1 minute. Pour into pie shell.

Spoon Brown Sugar Meringue onto hot pie filling; spread over filling, sealing meringue to edge of crust to prevent shrinking or weeping. Bake until delicate brown, about 10 minutes. Cool away from draft.

Coconut Cream Pie

9-inch Baked Pie Shell (page 28)
⅔ cup sugar
¼ cup cornstarch
½ teaspoon salt
3 cups milk
4 egg yolks, slightly beaten
2 tablespoons butter or margarine,
  softened
2 teaspoons vanilla
¾ cup flaked coconut
Sweetened whipped cream
¼ cup flaked coconut

Bake pie shell. Cool. Mix sugar, cornstarch and salt in medium saucepan. Gradually stir in milk. Cook over medium heat, stirring constantly, until mixture thickens and boils. Boil and stir 1 minute. Gradually stir at least half of the hot mixture into egg yolks. Blend into hot mixture in pan. Boil and stir 1 minute. Remove from heat; stir in butter and vanilla. Stir in ¾ cup coconut. Pour into pie shell; press plastic wrap onto filling. Refrigerate at least 2 hours. Top pie with whipped cream and sprinkle with ¼ cup coconut.

BANANA CREAM PIE: Increase vanilla to 1 tablespoon plus 1 teaspoon and omit coconut. Cover filling in saucepan with waxed paper; cool to room temperature. Arrange a layer of sliced bananas (2 large) ½ inch deep in baked pie shell; pour in cooled filling.

...olate Brownie Pie

Pastry for 9-inch One-Crust Pie (page 28)
2 tablespoons margarine or butter
2 ounces unsweetened chocolate
1/2 cup sugar
3/4 cup dark corn syrup
3 eggs
1 cup pecan halves

Heat oven to 375°. Prepare pastry. Heat margarine and chocolate over low heat until melted; cool. Beat chocolate mixture, sugar, corn syrup and eggs with hand beater. Stir in pecans. Pour into pastry-lined pie plate.

Bake just until set, 40 to 50 minutes. Refrigerate until chilled, at least 2 hours. Serve with sweetened whipped cream, if desired. Refrigerate any remaining pie immediately.

Kentucky Pecan Pie

8 SERVINGS

Pastry for 9-inch One-Crust Pie (page 28)
2/3 cup sugar
1/3 cup margarine or butter, melted
1 cup corn syrup
2 tablespoons bourbon
1/2 teaspoon salt
3 eggs
1 cup pecan halves or broken pecans
1 cup semisweet chocolate chips

Heat oven to 375°. Prepare pastry. Beat sugar, margarine, corn syrup, bourbon, salt and eggs with hand beater. Stir in pecans and chocolate chips. Pour into pastry-lined pie plate. Bake until set, 40 to 50 minutes. Refrigerate until chilled, at least 2 hours. Immediately refrigerate any remaining pie.

BRANDY PECAN PIE: Decrease corn syrup to 3/4 cup. Substitute 1/4 cup brandy for the bourbon and omit chocolate chips.

CHOCOLATE PECAN PIE: Melt 2 ounces unsweetened chocolate with the margarine. Omit bourbon and chocolate chips.

PECAN PIE: Omit bourbon and chocolate chips.

Sweet Potato Pie

Pastry for 9-inch One-Crust pie (page 28)
2 eggs
³/₄ cup sugar
1 teaspoon ground cinnamon
¹/₂ teaspoon salt
¹/₂ teaspoon ground ginger
¹/₄ teaspoon ground cloves
1 can (23 ounces) sweet potatoes, drained and mashed (1³/₄ to 2 cups)
1 can (12 ounces) evaporated milk

Heat oven to 425°. Prepare pastry. Beat eggs slightly in 2-quart bowl with hand beater; beat in remaining ingredients. Place pastry-lined pie plate on oven rack; pour sweet potato mixture into plate. Bake 15 minutes.

Reduce oven temperature to 350°. Bake until knife inserted in center comes out clean, 45 to 50 minutes. Refrigerate until chilled, at least 4 hours. Serve with sweetened whipped cream, if desired. Immediately refrigerate any remaining pie.

PRALINE SWEET POTATO PIE: Decrease second bake time to 35 minutes. Mix ¹/₃ cup packed brown sugar, ¹/₃ cup chopped pecans and 1 tablespoon margarine or butter, softened; sprinkle over pie. Bake until knife inserted in center comes out clean, about 10 minutes longer.

French Silk Tart

1 cup granulated sugar
³/₄ cup margarine or butter, softened
1¹/₂ teaspoons instant coffee
1¹/₂ teaspoons vanilla
¹/₄ teaspoon cream of tartar
3 ounces unsweetened chocolate, melted and cooled
3 eggs
10-inch baked tart shell or 9-inch Baked Pie Shell (page 28)
1 cup chilled whipping cream
2 tablespoons powdered sugar

Beat sugar and margarine in small bowl until light and fluffy. Stir in coffee (dry), vanilla, cream of tartar and chocolate. Beat in eggs until light and fluffy, about 3 minutes. Pour into tart shell. Refrigerate until set, 3 to 4 hours. Or cover with plastic wrap and freeze at least 8 hours.

If tart is frozen, remove from freezer 15 minutes before serving. Beat whipping cream and powdered sugar in chilled small bowl until stiff. Top tart with whipped cream.

Following pages: Sweet Potato Pie

Honey-Wine Cranberry Tart

8 TO 10 SERVINGS

Cookie Crust (below)
⅓ cup orange marmalade
½ cup coarsely chopped walnuts
1 envelope unflavored gelatin
¼ cup cold water
1 cup sauvignon blanc or dry white wine
½ cup honey
1 package (12 ounces) fresh cranberries
Sweetened whipped cream

Heat oven to 375°. Prepare Cookie Crust. Press in bottom and 1½ inches up side of ungreased springform pan, 9 × 3 inches. Bake until crust is set and light brown, 18 to 20 minutes. Spread orange marmalade on bottom; sprinkle with nuts.

Sprinkle gelatin on cold water in 3-quart saucepan. Let stand until gelatin is softened, about 5 minutes. Stir in remaining ingredients except whipped cream. Heat to boiling; reduce heat slightly. Boil uncovered 5 minutes. Cool 15 minutes.

Pour cranberry mixture over nuts in crust. Cover and refrigerate until chilled, at least 4 hours. Remove side of pan. Serve with sweetened whipped cream.

COOKIE CRUST

1¾ cups all-purpose flour
½ cup powdered sugar
¾ cup margarine or butter, softened

Mix all ingredients until crumbly; mix with hands until dough forms.

Peach-Pecan Tart

12 SERVINGS

Butter Crust (page 41)
Orange Glaze (page 41)
2 packages (3 ounces each) cream cheese, softened
4 cups sliced peaches (about 4 medium)
½ cup chopped pecans

Bake Butter Crust; cool. Prepare Orange Glaze. Beat cream cheese until smooth; spread on bottom of crust.

Arrange peaches on crust; sprinkle with pecans. Spoon Orange Glaze over top. Refrigerate until set, about 2 hours.

BUTTER CRUST

1 1/3 cups all-purpose flour
1/3 cup packed brown sugar
2/3 cup margarine or butter, softened

Heat oven to 400°. Mix flour and brown sugar; cut in margarine until crumbly. Press firmly and evenly against bottom and side of ungreased 12-inch pizza pan. Bake until light brown, 10 to 15 minutes.

ORANGE GLAZE

1 cup sugar
3 tablespoons cornstarch
1/4 teaspoon salt
1 cup orange juice
1/2 cup water

Mix sugar, cornstarch and salt in 1-quart saucepan. Gradually stir in orange juice and water. Heat to boiling over medium heat, stirring constantly. Boil and stir 1 minute; cool.

Lemon Fruit Tart

8 SERVINGS

Nut Crust (below)
1 teaspoon unflavored gelatin
1 tablespoon cold water
1/2 cup sugar
2 eggs
2 tablespoons grated lemon peel
1/4 cup lemon juice
1/2 cup whipping cream
1 cup strawberry halves
1 cup raspberries
1/2 cup blackberries or blueberries
1 mango or papaya, pared and sliced
1/3 cup guava jelly or apricot jam, melted

Prepare Nut Crust; cool. Sprinkle gelatin on cold water in 1½-quart saucepan to soften. Beat sugar and eggs until thick and lemon colored; stir into gelatin mixture. Heat just to boiling over low heat, stirring constantly, about 15 minutes. Remove from heat; stir in lemon peel and juice.

Beat whipping cream in chilled medium bowl until soft peaks form. Fold in lemon mixture; pour into Nut Crust. Refrigerate 2 hours. Arrange fruits on top; drizzle with jelly. Refrigerate any remaining tart.

NUT CRUST

1 cup all-purpose flour
1/2 cup finely chopped pecans
1/4 cup sugar
1/4 cup margarine or butter, softened
1 egg

Heat oven to 375°. Mix flour, pecans and sugar; mix in margarine and egg until crumbly. Press in bottom and up side of greased tart pan, 9 × 1 inch. Bake until light golden brown, 15 to 20 minutes.

Brown Sugar Pear Tart

6 TO 8 SERVINGS

Pecan Crust (below)
3 or 4 medium pears (about 2 pounds),
*   pared*
1/2 cup packed brown sugar
1 tablespoon all-purpose flour
1/2 teaspoon ground cinnamon
1 tablespoon margarine or butter

Bake Pecan Crust. Cut each pear lengthwise into halves; remove core. Place each pear half, cut side down, on cutting surface. Cut crosswise into thin slices. With spatula, lift each pear half and arrange on crust, separating and overlapping slices (retain pear shape) to cover surface of crust.

Mix brown sugar, flour, cinnamon and margarine; sprinkle over pears. Bake in 375° oven until crust is golden brown and pears are tender, 15 to 20 minutes.

PECAN CRUST

1 1/3 cups all-purpose flour
1/3 cup packed brown sugar
1/3 cup finely chopped pecans
1/2 teaspoon ground nutmeg
1/2 teaspoon grated lemon peel
2/3 cup margarine or butter, softened

Heat oven to 375°. Mix all ingredients except margarine; cut in margarine until crumbly. Press firmly and evenly against bottom and side of ungreased 12-inch pizza pan. Bake 8 minutes.

Blueberry Cobbler

6 SERVINGS

1/2 cup sugar
1 tablespoon cornstarch
4 cups blueberries
1 teaspoon lemon juice
3 tablespoons shortening
1 cup all-purpose flour
1 tablespoon sugar
1 1/2 teaspoons baking powder
1/2 teaspoon salt
1/2 cup milk

Heat oven to 400°. Mix 1/2 cup sugar and the cornstarch in 2-quart saucepan. Stir in blueberries and lemon juice. Cook, stirring constantly, until mixture thickens and boils. Boil and stir 1 minute. Pour into ungreased 2-quart casserole; keep blueberry mixture hot in oven.

Cut shortening into flour, 1 tablespoon sugar, the baking powder and salt until mixture resembles fine crumbs. Stir in milk. Drop dough by 6 spoonfuls onto hot blueberry mixture.

Bake until topping is golden brown, 25 to 30 minutes. Serve warm.

CHERRY COBBLER: Substitute 4 cups pitted red tart cherries for the blueberries; increase ½ cup sugar in cherry mixture to 1¼ cups, cornstarch to 3 tablespoons, and add ¼ teaspoon ground cinnamon with the cornstarch. Substitute ¼ teaspoon almond extract for the 1 teaspoon lemon juice.

PLUM COBBLER: Substitute 4 cups sliced plums (about 14 large) for the blueberries; increase sugar in plum mixture to ¾ cup, cornstarch to 3 tablespoons, and add ½ teaspoon ground cinnamon with the cornstarch.

Peach Cobbler with Caramel Sauce

8 SERVINGS

¼ cup packed brown sugar
1 tablespoon lemon juice
½ teaspoon ground cinnamon
3 pounds peaches, sliced, or 2 packages
    (16 ounces each) frozen sliced peaches,
    thawed and drained
¾ cup all-purpose flour
½ cup granulated sugar
2 teaspoons baking powder
¼ teaspoon salt
¾ cup whipping cream
¼ cup margarine or butter, melted
Caramel Sauce (below)

CARAMEL SAUCE

1 cup packed brown sugar
½ cup whipping cream
¼ cup corn syrup
1 tablespoon margarine or butter
2 teaspoons ground cinnamon

Heat oven to 375°. Mix brown sugar, lemon juice, cinnamon and peaches; place in greased shallow 2½-quart casserole. Mix flour, granulated sugar, baking powder and salt; stir in whipping cream and margarine until well blended. Spoon batter over fruit.

Bake until crust is deep golden brown, 40 to 45 minutes. Prepare Caramel Sauce. Serve with warm cobbler.

Heat all ingredients to boiling over medium heat, stirring constantly; reduce heat to low. Simmer uncovered 5 minutes.

Following pages: Peach Cobbler with Caramel Sauce

Mixed Fruit Cobbler

1 cup sugar
3 tablespoons cornstarch
¾ teaspoon ground cinnamon
3 cups sliced peeled peaches or nectar-
  ines (5 to 6 medium)
2 cups sliced unpeeled red plums
  (6 to 8 large)
1 cup blueberries
1 cup all-purpose flour
2 tablespoons sugar
1½ teaspoons baking powder
½ teaspoon salt
⅓ cup shortening
3 tablespoons milk
1 egg

Heat oven to 375°. Mix 1 cup sugar, the corn-starch and cinnamon in 3-quart saucepan. Stir in peaches and plums. Cook, stirring constantly, until mixture thickens and boils. Boil and stir 1 minute. Stir in blueberries. Pour into un-greased baking dish, 8 × 8 × 2 inches.

Mix flour, 2 tablespoons sugar, the baking powder and salt. Cut in shortening. Mix in milk and egg. Drop dough by 9 spoonfuls onto hot fruit mixture. Bake until topping is golden brown, 25 to 30 minutes. Serve with cream or ice cream, if desired.

Note: Other combinations of fresh fruit total-ing 6 cups can be substituted (purple plums, berries, cut-up rhubarb, cherries).

·3·

MOUSSES AND MOLDED CREAMS

Mango Mousse

½ cup sugar
2 envelopes unflavored gelatin
4 eggs
3 egg yolks
*2 cups mashed ripe mangoes (about
  3 mangoes)*
¼ cup brandy
¼ teaspoon almond extract
2 cups chilled whipping cream
Sweetened whipped cream

Mix sugar and gelatin in 2-quart saucepan. Beat eggs and egg yolks until thick and lemon colored, about 5 minutes.

Stir eggs into gelatin mixture. Heat just to boiling over medium heat, stirring constantly. Remove from heat; stir in mangoes, brandy and almond extract. Refrigerate just until gelatin mixture mounds slightly when dropped from a spoon, about 1½ hours.

Beat whipping cream in chilled large bowl until stiff. Fold mango mixture into whipped cream. Pour into 8-cup mold. Refrigerate until firm, about 4 hours; unmold. Serve with sweetened whipped cream. Garnish with mango slices, if desired.

APRICOT MOUSSE: Substitute 1 can (30 ounces) apricot halves, drained, for the mangoes. Place apricots in blender container; cover and blend on high speed until smooth, about 1 minute. Decrease sugar to ¼ cup.

Peach Mousse with Raspberry-Currant Sauce

6 SERVINGS

Raspberry-Currant Sauce (below)
2 large peaches, peeled and cut up (about
    2 cups)
1/2 teaspoon grated lemon peel
2 tablespoons lemon juice
1 envelope unflavored gelatin
1 egg white
1/8 teaspoon cream of tartar
1/8 teaspoon salt
1/4 cup sugar
1/2 cup chilled whipping cream

Prepare Raspberry-Currant Sauce. Place peaches, lemon peel and lemon juice in food processor workbowl fitted with steel blade or in blender container. Cover and process until peach mixture is smooth.

Pour into 1½-quart saucepan. Sprinkle with gelatin; let stand 1 minute to soften. Heat over low heat, stirring constantly, until gelatin is dissolved. Remove from heat; place saucepan in bowl of ice and water or refrigerate, stirring occasionally, until mixture mounds slightly when dropped from a spoon, about 15 minutes.

Beat egg white, cream of tartar and salt in medium bowl until foamy. Beat in sugar, 1 tablespoon at a time; continue beating until stiff and glossy. Fold in peach mixture.

Beat whipping cream in chilled small bowl until stiff; fold into peach mixture. Cover and refrigerate at least 2 hours but no longer than 24 hours.

Spoon into dessert dishes; serve with sauce. Garnish with additional fresh fruit, if desired. Refrigerate any remaining dessert.

RASPBERRY-CURRANT SAUCE

1/2 cup currant jelly
2 teaspoons cornstarch
1 cup fresh or loose pack frozen
    raspberries

Mix jelly and cornstarch in 1-quart saucepan; stir in raspberries. Heat to boiling, stirring constantly. Boil and stir 1 minute. Press through sieve to remove seeds. Cool at room temperature.

Chocolate Mousse

8 SERVINGS (ABOUT ½ CUP EACH)

4 ounces semisweet chocolate, cut into pieces
3 eggs, separated
1 teaspoon vanilla
¾ teaspoon cream of tartar
½ cup sugar
1 cup chilled whipping cream

Heat chocolate in heavy saucepan over low heat, stirring occasionally, until chocolate is melted. Remove from heat. Beat egg yolks slightly; stir yolks and vanilla into melted chocolate. Beat egg whites and cream of tartar in 2½-quart bowl until foamy. Beat in sugar, 1 tablespoon at a time; continue beating until stiff and glossy. Stir about ¼ of the meringue into chocolate mixture. Fold into remaining meringue.

Beat whipping cream in chilled small bowl until stiff. Fold into chocolate mixture. Spoon into dessert dishes. Refrigerate at least 2 hours. Top each serving with additional sweetened whipped cream and grated chocolate, if desired.

BRANDY CHOCOLATE MOUSSE: Fold in 2 tablespoons brandy with the whipped cream.

Orange Bavarian Cream

6 TO 8 SERVINGS

1 cup boiling water
1 package (3 ounces) orange-flavored gelatin
½ cup sugar
1 tablespoon grated orange peel
1 cup orange juice
1 cup chilled whipping cream

Pour boiling water over gelatin in bowl; stir until gelatin is dissolved. Stir in sugar, orange peel and juice. Refrigerate, stirring occasionally, until mixture mounds slightly when dropped from a spoon.

In chilled small bowl, beat whipping cream until stiff. Beat gelatin mixture until foamy. Fold in whipped cream. Pour into 4-cup mold or 6 to 8 dessert dishes or molds. Refrigerate until firm, about 4 hours. Unmold on serving plate.

Following pages: Peach Mousse with Raspberry-Currant Sauce

Berry Pirouette

1¾ cups boiling water

2 packages (3 ounces each) raspberry-flavored gelatin

1 package (16 ounces) frozen boysenberries, partially thawed

2 cups chilled whipping cream

1 package (5½ ounces) tubular pirouette cookies (about 24)

Pour boiling water on gelatin in large bowl; stir until gelatin is dissolved. Reserve 3 to 5 berries for garnish. Place remaining berries in food processor workbowl fitted with steel blade or in blender container. Cover and process until berry mixture is smooth. Stir berries into gelatin. Refrigerate until very thick but not set, about 1 hour.

Beat gelatin mixture on high speed until thick and fluffy, about 4 minutes. Beat 1 cup of the whipping cream in chilled large bowl until stiff; fold into gelatin mixture. Pour into springform pan, 9 × 3 inches. Refrigerate until set, about 3 hours.

Run knife around edge of dessert to loosen; remove side of pan. Place dessert on serving plate. Beat remaining whipping cream in chilled bowl until stiff. Spread side of dessert with half of the whipped cream.

Carefully cut cookies crosswise into halves. Arrange cookies, cut sides down, vertically around side of dessert; press lightly. Garnish with remaining whipped cream and berries.

PEACH PIROUETTE: Substitute 1 package (16 ounces) frozen sliced peaches, partially thawed, for the boysenberries and orange-flavored gelatin for the raspberry-flavored gelatin. Reserve 3 peach slices for garnish.

Fudge Soufflé

½ cup sugar
1¾ cups ruby port or sweet red wine
¼ teaspoon salt
2 envelopes unflavored gelatin
6 eggs, separated
1 package (12 ounces) semisweet choco-
*   late chips*
½ cup sugar
1½ cups chilled whipping cream

Make a 3-inch band of double-thickness aluminum foil 2 inches longer than the circumference of 1½-quart soufflé dish. Secure band around edge of dish.

Mix ½ cup sugar, the port, salt and gelatin in 2-quart saucepan. Beat egg yolks slightly; stir yolks and chocolate chips into gelatin mixture. Heat just to boiling over medium heat, stirring constantly; remove from heat.

Refrigerate, stirring occasionally, just until mixture mounds slightly when dropped from a spoon, 20 to 30 minutes. (If mixture becomes too thick, place pan in bowl of hot water; stir constantly until of proper consistency.)

Beat egg whites in large bowl until foamy. Beat in ½ cup sugar, 1 tablespoon at a time; continue beating until stiff and glossy. Do not underbeat. Fold gelatin mixture into egg whites.

Beat whipping cream in chilled medium bowl until stiff. Fold into egg-white mixture. Carefully turn into soufflé dish. Refrigerate until set, about 8 hours.

Just before serving, run knife around inside of foil band and carefully remove band. Refrigerate any remaining soufflé.

Lemon Soufflé

¾ cup sugar
1 cup water
¾ cup lemon juice (3 to 4 lemons)
¼ teaspoon salt
2 envelopes unflavored gelatin
4 eggs, separated
2 teaspoons grated lemon peel
¾ cup sugar
2 cups chilled whipping cream

Make a 4-inch band of triple-thickness aluminum foil 2 inches longer than circumference of 6-cup soufflé dish. Extend dish by securing band around outside edge. (A 2-quart round casserole can be used instead of soufflé dish and foil band.)

Mix ¾ cup sugar, the water, lemon juice, salt and gelatin in saucepan. Beat egg yolks slightly; stir into gelatin mixture. Heat just to boiling over medium heat, stirring constantly; remove from heat. Stir in lemon peel. Place pan in bowl of ice and water, or refrigerate, stirring occasionally, just until mixture mounds slightly when dropped from a spoon, 20 to 30 minutes. If mixture becomes too thick, place pan in bowl of hot water; stir constantly until mixture is of proper consistency.

Beat egg whites in 2½-quart bowl until foamy. Beat in ¾ cup sugar, 1 tablespoon at a time; continue beating until stiff and glossy. Do not underbeat. Fold gelatin mixture into egg whites.

Beat whipping cream in chilled large bowl until stiff. Fold whipped cream into egg-white mixture. Carefully turn into soufflé dish. Refrigerate until set, about 8 hours.

Just before serving, carefully remove foil band. Refrigerate any remaining soufflé immediately.

Lemon Schaum Torte

Meringue Shell (below)
³/₄ cup sugar
3 tablespoons cornstarch
¹/₄ teaspoon salt
³/₄ cup water
3 egg yolks, slightly beaten
1 tablespoon margarine or butter
1 teaspoon grated lemon peel
¹/₃ cup lemon juice
1 cup chilled whipping cream

Bake Meringue Shell. Mix sugar, cornstarch and salt in 2-quart saucepan. Gradually stir in water. Cook over medium heat, stirring constantly, until mixture thickens and boils. Boil and stir 1 minute. Stir at least half the thickened hot mixture gradually into egg yolks; stir into hot mixture in saucepan. Boil and stir 1 minute; remove from heat.

Stir in margarine, lemon peel and lemon juice. Cool to room temperature. Spoon into shell. Refrigerate at least 12 hours.

Beat whipping cream in chilled small bowl until stiff; spread over filling. Refrigerate any remaining dessert immediately.

MERINGUE SHELL

3 egg whites
¹/₄ teaspoon cream of tartar
³/₄ cup sugar

Heat oven to 275°. Cover cookie sheet with heavy brown paper. Beat egg whites and cream of tartar in 1½-quart bowl until foamy. Beat in sugar, 1 tablespoon at a time; continue beating until stiff and glossy. Do not underbeat. Shape meringue on brown paper into 9-inch circle with back of spoon, building up side.

Bake 1½ hours. Turn off oven; leave meringue in oven with door closed 1 hour. Finish cooling meringue at room temperature.

LIME SCHAUM TORTE: Substitute grated lime peel and lime juice for the lemon peel and lemon juice. Stir in 1 or 2 drops green food color.

Following pages: Lemon Soufflé, left, and Lemon Schaum Torte, right

Pavlova

3 egg whites
¼ teaspoon cream of tartar
¾ cup sugar
½ teaspoon vanilla
1 cup chilled whipping cream
2 tablespoons sugar
3 kiwifruit, pared and sliced*

Heat oven to 225°. Line bottom of round pan, 8 or 9 × 1½ inches, with brown paper. Beat egg whites and cream of tartar until foamy. Beat in ¾ cup sugar, 1 tablespoon at a time, and the vanilla; continue beating until stiff and glossy. Do not underbeat. Spread in pan. Bake 1½ hours. Turn off oven; leave meringue in oven with door closed 1 hour. Finish cooling meringue at room temperature.

Loosen edge of layer with knife; hit pan sharply on table to remove meringue. Invert on plate. (Meringue will be crumbly on bottom and around edge.) Remove paper. Beat whipping cream and 2 tablespoons sugar in chilled small bowl until stiff. Frost side and top of meringue with whipped cream, building up edge slightly. Arrange kiwifruit on top. Cut into wedges.

*1½ to 2 cups fresh strawberries, cut into halves, raspberries, blueberries or combination of these can be substituted for the kiwifruit.

· 4 ·

PUDDINGS AND CUSTARDS

Chocolate Ranch Pudding

8 TO 10 SERVINGS

¼ cup margarine or butter
2 ounces semisweet chocolate
1 cup packed brown sugar
¾ cup corn syrup
¼ cup bourbon
3 eggs, slightly beaten
1½ cups chopped pecans, toasted
1 cup chilled whipping cream
1 teaspoon bourbon, if desired

Heat oven to 400°. Heat margarine and chocolate in 1½-quart saucepan over low heat, stirring constantly, until chocolate is melted and mixture is smooth. Remove from heat; stir in brown sugar, corn syrup, ¼ cup bourbon and the eggs.

Sprinkle pecans over bottom of greased 2-quart casserole; pour chocolate mixture over pecans. Bake uncovered 10 minutes. Reduce oven temperature to 350°. Bake until pudding is set, 20 to 25 minutes longer.

Beat whipping cream in chilled small bowl until stiff; fold in 1 teaspoon bourbon. Serve pudding warm with whipped cream.

Steamed Molasses Pudding with Lemon Sauce

6 SERVINGS

1 egg
2 tablespoons shortening
1/2 cup boiling water
1/2 cup molasses
1 1/3 cups all-purpose flour
2 tablespoons sugar
1 teaspoon baking soda
1/4 teaspoon salt
Lemon Sauce (below)

Beat egg in 1½-quart bowl on high speed until very thick and lemon colored, about 5 minutes. Heat shortening in boiling water until melted. Beat shortening mixture, molasses, flour, sugar, baking soda and salt into egg on low speed. Pour into well-greased 4-cup mold. Cover tightly with aluminum foil.

Place mold on rack in Dutch oven or steamer; pour boiling water into Dutch oven halfway up mold. Cover Dutch oven. Keep water boiling over low heat until wooden pick inserted in center of pudding comes out clean, about 1½ hours.

Prepare Lemon Sauce. Remove mold from Dutch oven and let stand 5 minutes; unmold. Serve warm with Lemon Sauce.

LEMON SAUCE

1/2 cup sugar
2 tablespoons cornstarch
1 cup water
2 tablespoons margarine or butter
1 tablespoon grated lemon peel
1 tablespoon lemon juice

Mix sugar and cornstarch in saucepan. Gradually stir in water. Cook over medium heat, stirring constantly, until mixture thickens and boils. Boil and stir 1 minute; remove from heat. Stir in remaining ingredients. Serve warm or cool.

Steamed Chocolate Pudding with Hard Sauce

8 SERVINGS

1 cup sugar
2 tablespoons margarine or butter,
  softened
1 egg
2 ounces unsweetened chocolate, melted
1¾ cups all-purpose flour
1 teaspoon salt
¼ teaspoon cream of tartar
¼ teaspoon baking soda
1 cup milk
Hard Sauce (below)

Beat sugar, margarine, egg and chocolate in 1½-quart bowl with hand beater until blended. Mix remaining ingredients except milk and Hard Sauce; stir into chocolate mixture alternately with milk. Pour into greased 4-cup mold. Cover tightly with aluminum foil.

Prepare Hard Sauce. Place mold on rack in Dutch oven or steamer; pour boiling water into Dutch oven halfway up mold. Cover Dutch oven. Keep water boiling over low heat until wooden pick inserted in center of pudding comes out clean, about 2 hours.

Remove mold from Dutch oven and let stand 5 minutes; unmold. Serve hot with Hard Sauce.

HARD SAUCE

½ cup margarine or butter, softened
1 cup powdered sugar
2 teaspoons vanilla or 1 tablespoon
  brandy

Beat margarine on high speed until fluffy and light, about 5 minutes. Gradually beat in powdered sugar. Stir in vanilla. Refrigerate 1 hour.

Danish Berry Pudding

6 SERVINGS

1 package (10 ounces) frozen raspberries, thawed
1 package (10 ounces) frozen strawberries, thawed
¼ cup cornstarch
2 tablespoons sugar
½ cup cold water
1 tablespoon lemon juice
Slivered almonds

Purée berries in blender or press through sieve. Mix cornstarch and sugar in 1½-quart saucepan. Gradually stir in water; add purée. Heat to boiling, stirring constantly. Boil and stir 1 minute. Remove from heat; stir in lemon juice. Pour into dessert dishes or serving bowl. Cover and refrigerate at least 2 hours. Sprinkle with almonds; serve with half-and-half, if desired.

Following pages: Steamed Molasses Pudding with Lemon Sauce

Russian Apricot Pudding

2 cups water
1 cup dried apricot halves (6 ounces)
1/4 cup sugar
3 tablespoons cornstarch
Dash of salt

Heat water and apricots to boiling; reduce heat. Cover and simmer until tender, about 20 minutes. Place apricots and 1/2 cup cooking liquid in blender container; cover and purée until uniform consistency. Press through sieve.

Mix sugar, cornstarch and salt in 1 1/2-quart saucepan; gradually stir in apricot purée and remaining cooking liquid. Heat to boiling over medium heat, stirring constantly. Boil and stir 1 minute. Pour into dessert dishes. Serve with half-and-half or sweetened whipped cream, if desired.

Coconut-Raisin Pudding

3 cups shredded fresh coconut
1 cup sugar
2 cups milk
Dash of salt
3 eggs, beaten
1/2 cup raisins
3 tablespoons rum

Heat coconut, sugar, milk and salt to boiling in 3-quart saucepan over medium heat, stirring frequently. Stir at least half of the hot mixture gradually into eggs. Blend into hot mixture in saucepan. Cook over low heat, stirring constantly, until mixture is thickened, 5 to 8 minutes. Remove from heat; stir in raisins and rum. Serve warm or cold.

Chocolate Pots de Crème

4 OR 5 SERVINGS

²/₃ cup semisweet chocolate chips
1 cup half-and-half
2 eggs
3 tablespoons sugar
2 tablespoons rum, if desired
Dash of salt

Heat oven to 350°. Heat chocolate chips and half-and-half, stirring constantly, until chocolate is melted and mixture is smooth; cool slightly. Beat remaining ingredients; gradually stir into chocolate mixture. Pour into 4 or 5 ovenproof pot de crème cups or 4 ungreased 6-ounce custard cups.

Place cups in baking pan on oven rack. Pour boiling water into pan to within ½ inch of tops of cups. Bake 20 minutes; cool slightly. Cover and refrigerate at least 4 hours but no longer than 24 hours. Refrigerate any remaining pudding immediately.

Bread Pudding with Whiskey Sauce

8 SERVINGS

2 cups milk
¼ cup margarine or butter
½ cup sugar
1 teaspoon ground cinnamon or nutmeg
¼ teaspoon salt
2 eggs, slightly beaten
6 cups dry bread cubes (8 slices bread)
½ cup raisins, if desired
Whiskey Sauce (below)

Heat oven to 350°. Heat milk and margarine over medium heat until margarine is melted and milk is scalded. Mix sugar, cinnamon, salt and eggs in 3-quart bowl; stir in bread cubes and raisins. Stir in milk mixture; pour into ungreased 1½-quart casserole. Place casserole in pan of very hot water (1 inch deep). Bake until knife inserted 1 inch from edge of casserole comes out clean, 40 to 45 minutes. Prepare Whiskey Sauce; serve with warm bread pudding.

WHISKEY SAUCE

1 cup packed brown sugar
½ cup margarine or butter
3 to 4 tablespoons bourbon

Heat brown sugar, margarine and bourbon to boiling in 1-quart heavy saucepan over medium heat, stirring constantly.

PUDDINGS AND CUSTARDS   65

Chocolate Terrine

1 package (3½ ounces) almond paste
1½ cups half-and-half
4 ounces semisweet chocolate, coarsely
    chopped
4 ounces white chocolate (vanilla-flavored
    candy coating), coarsely chopped
4 eggs, slightly beaten
2 tablespoons brandy
Chocolate Glaze (page 67)
1 to 2 tablespoons powdered sugar

Line loaf pan, 8½ × 4½ × 2½ inches, with aluminum foil, leaving about 2 inches overhanging sides. Roll almond paste between 2 sheets waxed paper into rectangle, 8 × 4 inches; cover with plastic wrap and set aside.

Heat oven to 350°. Heat half-and-half, semisweet chocolate and white chocolate over low heat, stirring constantly, until chocolates are melted and mixture is smooth; cool slightly. Gradually stir eggs and brandy into chocolate mixture. Pour into lined pan.

Place pan in pan of very hot water (1 inch deep) in oven. Bake until knife inserted halfway between edge and center comes out clean, 40 to 50 minutes. Remove from water. Remove waxed paper from almond paste and immediately place on hot terrine; cool 1 hour. Cover and refrigerate at least 6 hours but no longer than 24 hours.

Prepare Chocolate Glaze; reserve ¼ cup. Remove terrine from pan by inverting on serving plate. Carefully remove foil. Spread remaining glaze evenly and smoothly over sides and top of terrine.

Stir 1 to 2 tablespoons powdered sugar into reserved chocolate glaze until smooth and of desired consistency. Place in decorating bag with small writing tip or small sturdy plastic storage bag. (If using plastic bag, cut off very small corner of bag, about ⅛ inch in diameter.) Write *Terrine* on top and decorate around edges of top with remaining chocolate. To serve, cut into 8 slices, about 1 inch each; cut slices into halves. Refrigerate any remaining terrine.

CHOCOLATE GLAZE

1 cup semisweet chocolate chips
1/4 cup margarine or butter
2 tablespoons corn syrup

Heat chocolate chips, margarine and corn syrup over low heat, stirring constantly, until chocolate is melted; cool.

Crème Brûlée

4 egg yolks
3 tablespoons granulated sugar
2 cups whipping cream
1/3 cup packed brown sugar
4 cups cut-up fresh fruit

Beat egg yolks in 1½-quart bowl on high speed until thick and lemon colored, about 5 minutes. Gradually beat in granulated sugar. Heat whipping cream in large saucepan over medium heat just until hot. Stir at least half of the hot cream gradually into egg yolk mixture; stir into hot cream in saucepan. Cook over low heat, stirring constantly, until mixture thickens, 5 to 8 minutes (do not boil). Pour custard into ungreased pie plate, 9 × 1¼ inches. Cover and refrigerate at least 2 hours but no longer than 24 hours.

Set oven control to broil and/or 550°. Sprinkle brown sugar over custard. Broil with top about 5 inches from heat until sugar is melted and forms a glaze, about 3 minutes. Spoon over fruit. Refrigerate any remaining sauce immediately.

Following pages: Chocolate Terrine

Baked Custard

3 eggs, slightly beaten
⅓ cup sugar
1 teaspoon vanilla
Dash of salt
2½ cups milk, scalded
Ground nutmeg

Heat oven to 350°. Mix eggs, sugar, vanilla and salt. Gradually stir in milk. Pour into six 6-ounce custard cups; sprinkle with nutmeg. Place cups in rectangular pan, 13 × 9 × 2 inches, on oven rack. Pour very hot water into pan to within ½ inch of tops of cups.

Bake until knife inserted halfway between center and edge comes out clean, about 45 minutes. Remove cups from water. Serve warm or chilled. Refrigerate any remaining custards immediately.

CARAMEL CUSTARD: Before preparing custard, heat ½ cup sugar in heavy 1-quart saucepan over low heat, stirring constantly, until melted and golden brown. Divide syrup among custard cups; tilt cups to coat bottoms. Allow syrup to harden in cups about 10 minutes. Pour custard mixture over syrup; bake. Unmold and serve warm or, if desired, refrigerate and unmold at serving time. Caramel syrup will run down sides of custard, forming a sauce.

RASPBERRY CUSTARD: Mix ⅓ cup raspberry preserves and 1 tablespoon orange-flavored liqueur; divide among six 6-ounce custard cups. Continue as directed except mix in 1 teaspoon orange-flavored liqueur with the salt; omit nutmeg. Refrigerate and unmold at serving time. Serve with raspberries.

Wine Custard

4 egg yolks
1 egg
1/3 cup sugar
1/3 cup cream sherry or sweet red wine
Dash of salt

Beat egg yolks and egg in small bowl on high speed until thick and lemon colored, about 3 minutes. Gradually beat in sugar, scraping bowl occasionally. Beat in cream sherry and salt on low speed.

Pour mixture into top of double boiler. (A metal bowl placed over saucepan of simmering water can be substituted for double boiler.) Add hot water to bottom of double boiler but not enough to touch top. Cook mixture over medium heat, stirring constantly, until slightly thickened, about 5 minutes. (Water in double boiler should simmer but not boil.) Remove from heat. Serve immediately.

Almond Custard with Litchis

3/4 cup water
1/4 cup sugar
1 envelope unflavored gelatin
1 cup milk
1 teaspoon almond extract
2 cans (11 ounces each) litchis

Heat water, sugar and gelatin to boiling, stirring occasionally, until sugar and gelatin are dissolved. Remove from heat. Stir in milk and almond extract. Pour into loaf pan, 9 × 5 × 3 inches. Cover and refrigerate until firm, at least 4 hours.

Cut gelatin custard into 1-inch diamonds or squares. Place litchis (with syrup) in serving bowl; arrange custard around fruit.

Following pages: Almond Custard with Litchis

·5·
FROZEN DESSERTS

Pineapple Ice

*4 cups 1-inch pieces pineapple (about
  1 medium pineapple)*
½ cup light corn syrup
2 tablespoons lemon juice

Place all ingredients in blender container. Cover and blend on high speed until smooth, about 5 seconds. Pour into square baking dish, 8 × 8 × 2 inches or loaf pan, 9 × 5 × 3 inches. Freeze until firm around the edges but soft in center, about 2 hours. Spoon into blender container. Cover and blend on high speed until smooth. Pour into square baking dish or loaf pan. Freeze until firm, about 3 hours.

FOOD PROCESSOR DIRECTIONS: Place all ingredients in workbowl fitted with steel blade. Cover and process until smooth, about 10 seconds. Continue as directed.

CANTALOUPE ICE: Substitute 4 cups 1-inch pieces cantaloupe for the pineapple.

WATERMELON ICE: Substitute 4 cups 1-inch pieces watermelon for the pineapple.

Cranberry Ice

1 pound cranberries
2 cups water
2 cups sugar
1/4 cup lemon juice
1 teaspoon grated orange peel
2 cups cold water

Cook cranberries in 2 cups water until skins are broken, about 10 minutes. Rub cranberries through sieve to make smooth pulp. Stir in sugar, lemon juice and orange peel. Stir in 2 cups cold water. Pour into square baking dish, 8 × 8 × 2 inches. Freeze, stirring several times to keep mixture smooth, until firm. Let stand at room temperature 10 minutes before serving.

Gingered Pear Sorbet

1 can (29 ounces) pear halves, drained (reserve 1 cup syrup)
1/4 cup sugar
2 tablespoons lemon juice
1 to 1 1/2 teaspoons finely chopped crystallized ginger or 1/8 teaspoon ground ginger

Heat reserved pear syrup and sugar to boiling, stirring constantly; remove from heat. Cool. Place pears, half at a time, in blender container; cover and purée until uniform consistency. Mix syrup, purée, lemon juice and ginger; pour into freezer tray. Freeze until partially frozen, 1 to 1 1/2 hours.

Pour into blender; blend on medium speed until smooth and fluffy. Return to freezer tray. Freeze until firm, about 3 hours. Let stand at room temperature about 10 minutes before serving.

Strawberry Ice Cream

8 SERVINGS

3 egg yolks, beaten
½ cup sugar
1 cup milk
¼ teaspoon salt
2 cups chilled whipping cream
1 teaspoon vanilla
1 pint strawberries
½ cup sugar
Few drops red food color, if desired

Mix egg yolks, ½ cup sugar, the milk and salt. Cook over medium heat, stirring constantly, just until bubbles appear around edge. Refrigerate in chilled large bowl until room temperature, 2 to 3 hours.

Stir whipping cream and vanilla into milk mixture. Mash strawberries and ½ cup sugar; stir into milk mixture. Mix in food color.

Pour into freezer can; put dasher in place. Cover and adjust crank. Place can in freezer tub. Fill freezer tub ⅓ full of ice; add remaining ice alternately with layers of rock salt (6 parts ice to 1 part rock salt). Turn crank until it turns with difficulty. Drain water from freezer tub. Remove lid; take out dasher. Pack mixture down; replace lid. Repack in ice and rock salt. Let stand several hours to ripen.

CHOCOLATE ICE CREAM: Omit strawberries, ½ cup sugar and the food color. Increase sugar in cooked mixture to 1 cup. Beat 2 ounces unsweetened chocolate, melted, into milk mixture before cooking.

NUT BRITTLE ICE CREAM: Omit strawberries, ½ cup sugar and the food color. Increase vanilla to 1 tablespoon. Stir 1 cup crushed almond, pecan or peanut brittle into milk mixture after adding vanilla.

PEACH ICE CREAM: Omit strawberries and food color. Mash 4 or 5 peaches to yield 2 cups. Stir ½ cup sugar into peaches; stir into milk mixture after adding vanilla.

Honey–Vanilla Bean Ice Cream

8 SERVINGS

½ cup milk
½ cup honey
¼ teaspoon salt
3 egg yolks, beaten
1 vanilla bean (3 inches)
2 cups chilled whipping cream

CRANK-TYPE FREEZER DIRECTIONS: Mix milk, honey, salt, egg yolks and vanilla bean in saucepan. Cook over medium heat, stirring constantly, just until bubbles appear around edge. Remove vanilla bean; split bean lengthwise into halves. Scrape seeds into cooked mixture with tip of small knife; discard bean. Cool to room temperature. Stir in whipping cream.

Pour into freezer can; put dasher in place. Cover and adjust crank. Place can in freezer tub. Fill freezer tub ⅓ full of ice; add remaining ice alternately with layers of rock salt (6 parts ice to 1 part rock salt). Turn crank until it turns with difficulty. Drain water from freezer tub. Remove lid; take out dasher. Pack mixture down; replace lid. Repack in ice and rock salt. Let stand to ripen several hours.

REFRIGERATOR DIRECTIONS: Prepare custard mixture as directed above, except do not stir in whipping cream after cooling to room temperature.

Pour into square baking dish, 8 × 8 × 2 inches or loaf pan, 9 × 5 × 3 inches. Freeze until mixture is mushy and partially frozen, 1 to 2 hours. Beat whipping cream in chilled bowl until soft peaks form. Spoon partially frozen mixture into another chilled bowl; beat until smooth. Fold in whipped cream. Pour into 2 metal refrigerator trays or loaf pans, 9 × 5 × 3 inches. Cover to prevent crystals from forming. Freeze, stirring frequently during first hours, until firm, 4 to 5 hours.

Following pages: Gingered Pear Sorbet, left (page 75), and Honey–Vanilla Bean Ice Cream, right

Garden Apple Ice Cream

8 SERVINGS

3 egg yolks, beaten
1/2 cup sugar
1/2 cup milk
1/4 teaspoon salt
2 cups chilled whipping cream
3/4 cup frozen apple juice concentrate
   (6 ounces), thawed
1/2 to 1 teaspoon rose water
3 to 4 drops red food color, if desired

Mix egg yolks, sugar, milk and salt in 2-quart saucepan. Cook over medium heat, stirring constantly, just until bubbles appear around edge. Refrigerate in chilled large bowl until room temperature, 1 to 2 hours.

Stir remaining ingredients into milk mixture. Pour into freezer can; put dasher in place. Cover and adjust crank. Place can in freezer tub. Fill freezer tub 1/3 full of ice; add remaining ice alternately with layers of rock salt (6 parts ice to 1 part rock salt). Turn crank until it turns with difficulty. Drain water from freezer tub. Remove lid; take out dasher. Pack mixture down; replace lid. Repack in ice and salt. Let stand several hours to ripen.

Hawaiian Ice Cream Dessert

12 TO 16 SERVINGS

1 can (20 ounces) crushed pineapple in
   syrup
1 package (13¾ ounces) soft coconut
   macaroons, crumbled
1 half-gallon vanilla ice cream, softened
1/2 cup toasted chopped macadamia nuts
   or almonds
3/4 cup chilled whipping cream

Heat oven to 400°. Drain pineapple, reserving 1/4 cup syrup. Bake macroon crumbs uncovered, stirring occasionally, until golden brown, 8 to 10 minutes; cool completely.

Reserve 2 tablespoons macaroon crumbs. Mix remaining crumbs and the pineapple syrup in ungreased springform pan, 9 × 3 inches; press evenly on bottom and 1 inch up side of pan. Mix ice cream, nuts and pineapple; spread evenly in pan. Cover; freeze until firm, about 8 hours.

Run knife around edge of dessert to loosen; remove side of pan. Beat whipping cream in chilled small bowl until stiff. Spoon or pipe whipped cream on top of dessert; sprinkle with reserved macaroon crumbs.

Frozen Rum Charlotte with Chocolate Sauce

12 TO 16 SERVINGS

Chocolate Sauce (below)
17 ladyfingers
⅓ cup rum
3 tablespoons water
3 cups chilled whipping cream
¼ cup rum

Prepare Chocolate Sauce; cool. Reserve 1 cup sauce. Cover and refrigerate remaining sauce.

Cut ladyfingers lengthwise into halves. Mix ⅓ cup rum and the water; dip cut surface of each ladyfinger half into rum mixture. Place ladyfingers, cut surfaces facing toward inside, on bottom and upright around side of spring-form pan, 9 × 3 inches. Beat whipping cream in chilled large bowl until stiff. Mix reserved 1 cup Chocolate Sauce and ¼ cup rum; fold into whipping cream. Spoon into pan; smooth top. Freeze until firm, about 8 hours.

Remove from freezer and refrigerate at least 1 hour but no longer than 2 hours before serving. Unmold Charlotte. Heat remaining Chocolate Sauce, stirring occasionally, just until warm. Cut dessert into wedges; serve with Chocolate Sauce.

CHOCOLATE SAUCE

1 cup sugar
1 can (12 ounces) evaporated milk
1 package (12 ounces) semisweet choco-
*   late chips*
1 tablespoon margarine or butter
2 teaspoons rum

Heat sugar, milk and chocolate chips to boiling over medium heat, stirring constantly. Remove from heat; stir in margarine and rum.

Following pages: Frozen Rum Charlotte with Chocolate Sauce

Frozen Cherry Cream

2 cups pitted dark sweet cherries
1/4 cup light corn syrup
3 tablespoons cherry brandy
1 cup chilled whipping cream

Place cherries, corn syrup and brandy in workbowl of food processor fitted with steel blade or in blender container. Cover and process until coarsely chopped. Pour into square pan or baking dish, $9 \times 9 \times 2$ inches. Cover and freeze until partially frozen, about 1 hour.

Beat whipping cream in chilled medium bowl until stiff. Stir cherry mixture; fold into whipped cream. Pour into pan. Cover and freeze, stirring once, until firm, about 2 hours. Let stand 10 minutes before serving.

Frozen Lemon Cream

4 SERVINGS (ABOUT 1 CUP EACH)

2 cups chilled whipping cream
1 1/4 cups sugar
2 tablespoons grated lemon peel
1/3 cup lemon juice (about 1 1/2 lemons)
1 or 2 drops yellow food color

Beat all ingredients in chilled large bowl until stiff. Pour into square pan, $8 \times 8 \times 2$ inches. Freeze until firm, about 2 hours.

Creamy Pumpkin Squares

9 SERVINGS

1 1/4 cups graham cracker crumbs (about
*   16 squares)*
1/4 cup margarine or butter, melted
1 cup mashed cooked pumpkin
1/2 cup packed brown sugar
1/2 teaspoon salt
1/2 teaspoon ground cinnamon
1/2 teaspoon ground ginger
1/4 teaspoon ground nutmeg
1 quart vanilla ice cream, softened

Mix cracker crumbs and butter. Reserve 2 to 3 tablespoons crumb mixture; press remaining crumb mixture firmly and evenly in bottom of ungreased square pan, $9 \times 9 \times 2$ inches.

Beat pumpkin, sugar, salt and spices until well blended. Stir in ice cream. Pour into pan; sprinkle reserved crumb mixture over top. Freeze until firm, about 4 hours. Remove from freezer 10 to 15 minutes before serving.

Frozen Mocha-Almond Dessert

Almond Crunch (below)
7 egg yolks
½ cup corn syrup
½ cup semisweet chocolate chips, melted
  and cooled
1 teaspoon coffee-flavored liqueur
1 teaspoon freeze-dried coffee
1 teaspoon almond-flavored liqueur
2 cups chilled whipping cream

Prepare Almond Crunch. Beat egg yolks on high speed until thick and lemon colored, about 8 minutes. Stir in corn syrup. Pour mixture into 2-quart saucepan. Cook over medium heat, stirring constantly, until hot but not boiling, about 6 minutes. Cool to room temperature.

Place ⅓ of the egg yolk mixture in each of three 2-quart bowls. Stir melted chocolate chips into mixture in one bowl, coffee-flavored liqueur and coffee (dry) into mixture in another bowl and Almond Crunch and almond-flavored liqueur into remaining egg mixture.

Beat whipping cream in chilled large bowl until stiff. Fold ⅓ of the whipped cream into egg yolk mixture in each bowl.

Spread chocolate mixture in ungreased 7-inch springform pan; cover and freeze 30 minutes. Cover remaining bowls and refrigerate. After 30 minutes, spread Almond Crunch mixture over chocolate layer; cover and freeze 30 minutes. Spread coffee mixture over Almond Crunch layer; cover and freeze until firm, about 8 hours.

Loosen edge of Frozen Mocha-Almond Dessert with knife before removing side of pan. Return dessert to freezer until serving time. Garnish with chocolate curls, if desired.

ALMOND CRUNCH

3 tablespoons sugar
3 tablespoons toasted whole almonds

Cook sugar in 6- or 7-inch skillet over low heat, stirring constantly, until sugar melts and turns light brown. Stir in almonds. Pour into buttered shallow pan; cool. Break into pieces and crush.

· 6 ·

FRUIT AND NATURALLY SWEET DESSERTS

Honey Ambrosia

4 TO 6 SERVINGS

4 medium oranges, pared and thinly
  sliced
1 medium banana, sliced
1/2 cup orange juice
1/4 cup honey
2 tablespoons lemon juice
1/4 cup flaked coconut

Gently mix orange and banana slices. Mix orange juice, honey and lemon juice; pour over fruit. Sprinkle with coconut.

Sliced Oranges with Dates

4 TO 6 SERVINGS

4 large oranges, pared and sliced
1/3 cup pitted dates, cut into fourths
2 tablespoons toasted chopped almonds
1 to 2 tablespoons orange-flower water

Arrange orange slices on serving platter. Sprinkle with dates and almonds. Drizzle with orange-flower water. Cover and refrigerate at least 4 hours. Garnish with fresh mint leaves, if desired.

Oranges and Cinnamon

4 SERVINGS

4 large chilled oranges
Ground cinnamon
8 tablespoons coconut

Pare and thinly slice oranges. Arrange oranges on crushed ice on individual serving dishes. Just before serving, sprinkle each serving with ¼ teaspoon ground cinnamon and 2 tablespoons coconut.

Baked Maple Apples

4 SERVINGS

4 baking apples (Rome Beauty, Golden Delicious, Greening)
4 teaspoons margarine or butter
4 tablespoons maple or maple-flavored syrup

Core baking apples. Pare 1-inch strip of skin from around middle of each apple, or pare upper half of each to prevent splitting.

Place apples upright in ungreased baking dish. Place 1 teaspoon margarine and 1 tablespoon syrup in center of each apple. Pour water (¼ inch deep) into baking dish.

Bake uncovered in 375° oven until tender when pierced with fork, 30 to 40 minutes. (Time will vary with size and variety of apples.) Spoon syrup in dish over apples several times during baking. Serve with cream, if desired.

Pineapple with Port

4 SERVINGS

4 slices pineapple, each ½ inch thick
2 to 3 teaspoons sugar*
¼ cup ruby port or Madeira

Place each slice pineapple on dessert plate; sprinkle with sugar. Sprinkle 1 tablespoon of the port over each slice pineapple. Cover and refrigerate at least 4 hours. Garnish with fresh mint leaves, if desired.

*If pineapple is sweet, omit sugar.

Watermelon with Blackberries and Pear Purée

6 SERVINGS

3 slices medium watermelon, each 3/4 inch thick
1 1/2 cups blackberries
Pear Purée (below)

Cut each watermelon slice into 10 wedges. Cut rind from wedges; remove seeds. Arrange wedges on 6 dessert plates; top with blackberries. Top each serving with Pear Purée.

PEAR PURÉE

2 medium pears, pared
1/4 cup light rum

Cut pears into fourths and remove cores and stems. Place pears and rum in workbowl of food processor fitted with steel blade or in blender container. Cover and process until smooth, about 1 minute.

Gingered Pineapple

4 SERVINGS

1 pineapple (with green leaves)
1/4 cup dark rum
1 teaspoon ground ginger
1/2 cup flaked or shredded coconut

Cut pineapple lengthwise into halves through green top; cut each half into halves. Cut core from each quarter and cut along curved edges with grapefruit knife. Cut fruit crosswise into 3/4-inch slices; then cut lengthwise down center of slices. Mix rum and ginger; spoon over pineapple. Cover and refrigerate at least 4 hours but no longer than 24 hours.

About 15 minutes before serving, cook coconut in 8 × 8 × 2-inch baking pan in 350° oven, stirring occasionally, until golden brown, 8 to 10 minutes. Sprinkle over pineapple quarters. Garnish with strawberries and mint leaves, if desired.

Papaya Dessert

3 papayas
1/2 cup chilled whipping cream
2 tablespoons powdered sugar
2 tablespoons orange-flavored liqueur
1/2 lime
1 kiwifruit, sliced

Cut 2 of the papayas lengthwise into slices. Cut remaining papaya into pieces. Place papaya pieces in blender container. Cover and blend on high speed, stopping blender occasionally to scrape sides, until mixture is smooth, about 1 minute.

Beat whipping cream and powdered sugar in chilled small bowl until thick but not stiff. Fold in puréed papaya and liqueur. Arrange papaya slices on 4 plates; squeeze juice from lime over papaya. Spoon whipped cream mixture over papaya; top with kiwifruit.

CANTALOUPE DESSERT: Substitute 1 small cantaloupe for the 3 papayas. Cut 3/4 of the cantaloupe into slices. Cut remaining 1/4 into pieces. Place pieces in blender container and continue as directed.

Starfruit and Strawberries in Champagne

2 starfruit
1/4 cup sugar
2 cups strawberries, cut into halves
3/4 cup champagne or Catawba juice

Cut starfruit crosswise into 1/4-inch slices. Sprinkle with sugar; let stand 30 minutes.

Spoon starfruit and strawberries into dessert dishes. Pour champagne over fruit.

Following pages: Watermelon with Blackberries and Pear Purée

Peaches with Yogurt

4 SERVINGS

4 peaches, sliced
2 tablespoons wheat germ
1/4 teaspoon ground ginger
1 cup plain yogurt
1 tablespoon packed brown sugar
1/4 cup packed brown sugar

Toss peaches, wheat germ and ginger; divide among 4 dishes. Mix yogurt and 1 tablespoon brown sugar; spoon 1/4 cup yogurt mixture over fruit in each dish. Top with remaining brown sugar; sprinkle with granola, if desired.

BANANAS WITH YOGURT: Substitute 2 medium bananas, sliced, for the peaches. Sprinkle with ground nutmeg, if desired.

STRAWBERRIES WITH YOGURT: Substitute 1 pint strawberries, cut into halves, for the sliced peaches.

Tropical Fruit with Chocolate Sauce

6 TO 8 SERVINGS

Chocolate Sauce (below)
3 to 4 cups assorted fresh tropical fruit, cut up*
2 to 3 tablespoons orange-flavored liqueur or rum

Prepare Chocolate Sauce. Toss fruit and liqueur. Cover and refrigerate, stirring once or twice, at least 1 hour. Spoon fruit into dessert dishes; drizzle with Chocolate Sauce.

CHOCOLATE SAUCE

1 package (6 ounces) semisweet chocolate chips
1/2 cup evaporated milk
1/2 cup sugar
2 teaspoons margarine or butter
1 tablespoon orange-flavored liqueur or rum

Heat chocolate, evaporated milk and sugar to boiling over medium heat, stirring constantly; remove from heat. Stir in margarine and liqueur. Let stand 1 hour. Cover and refrigerate any remaining sauce.

*Suggested fruits are banana, pineapple, strawberries, papaya, mango and starfruit.

Pears Stuffed with Dates

¼ cup brandy
1 cup pitted dates
6 pears
2 cups water
⅓ cup sugar
1 stick cinnamon
4 whole cloves
¼ cup grenadine syrup
Juice of ½ lime (about 2 tablespoons)

Pour brandy over dates; let stand 2 hours. Pare and core pears (do not remove stems). Heat water, sugar, cinnamon and cloves in 3-quart saucepan, stirring occasionally, to boiling; reduce heat and add pears. Simmer uncovered, turning occasionally, until pears are soft but not mushy when pierced with a sharp knife, about 5 minutes. Remove pears with slotted spoon; cool.

Simmer syrup until reduced to ½ cup. Remove cinnamon and cloves. Stir in grenadine and lime juice. Fill pear cavities with dates. Place pears in serving dishes. Spoon about 2 tablespoons syrup onto each pear. Refrigerate until cold, at least 3 hours.

Strawberries Romanov

1 quart strawberries
½ cup powdered sugar
*3 to 4 tablespoons kirsch or orange-
flavored liqueur*
1 cup chilled whipping cream

Cut strawberries into halves, reserving 3 strawberries for garnish. Sprinkle with powdered sugar and kirsch; stir gently. Cover and refrigerate about 2 hours. Just before serving, beat whipping cream in chilled small bowl until soft peaks form; fold in strawberries. Garnish with reserved strawberries.

Following pages: Strawberries Romanov, left, and Papaya Dessert, right (page 89)

Meringue-topped Apples

4 tart cooking apples, pared and cut
  into thin slices
3 tablespoons margarine or butter, melted
2 tablespoons sugar
1/4 cup raisins or currants
1 tablespoon Calvados or applejack
3 egg whites
1/4 teaspoon cream of tartar
1/4 cup sugar

Arrange apples in greased square baking dish, 8 × 8 × 2 inches. Pour margarine over apples; sprinkle with 2 tablespoons sugar, the raisins and Calvados. Cover and cook in 350° oven until apples are tender, about 30 minutes.

Beat egg whites and cream of tartar on medium speed until foamy. Beat in 1/4 cup sugar, 1 tablespoon at a time; continue beating on high speed until stiff and glossy. Spread over apples. Bake until meringue is golden brown, 12 to 15 minutes.

Orange Dessert Omelets

2 eggs, separated
1/8 teaspoon cream of tartar
2 tablespoons granulated sugar
2 tablespoons water
2 tablespoons all-purpose flour
3 oranges, pared and sectioned
Powdered sugar

Beat egg whites and cream of tartar in large bowl until foamy. Gradually beat in 2 tablespoons granulated sugar; continue beating until stiff and glossy. Do not overbeat. Beat egg yolks and water until thick and lemon colored, about 5 minutes. Stir in flour. Fold egg yolk mixture into egg whites.

Heat oven to 400°. Grease and flour 2 round pans, 9 × 1 1/2 inches. Divide egg mixture between pans. Bake until puffy and light brown, 8 to 10 minutes. Remove omelets from pans; spoon half of the oranges onto half of each omelet. Fold other half of each omelet over oranges; sprinkle with powdered sugar. Garnish with orange sections, if desired.

RED SPOON TIPS

Everyone needs a little inspiration from time to time. Just turn through the preceding pages for more than one hundred inspired suggestions. If you want advice about how to decorate a dessert or make a professional-looking pie crust, if you have questions about how to make a smooth meringue or freeze a freshly baked cake to enjoy another day, read on for those tips and much more.

Decorating Desserts

- The simplest decoration is a dusting of powdered sugar. This works nicely on any fairly dry surface—a damp or wet one will melt the sugar—whether it is cake or pastry. To make a pretty design in powdered sugar, center a paper doily on the dessert surface, sift sugar over the doily, then remove the doily carefully, leaving a sugar design.
- Fresh mint sprigs are as delicious as they are attractive. Use them to adorn fresh fruit and dark chocolate desserts.

- Tiny, edible flower blossoms make unusual and colorful garnishes for desserts. They can be anchored in frosting, or placed simply on the rim of a plate. Arrange them on the dessert as close to serving time as possible. Once they are in place, most fresh blossoms will last two or three hours if the dessert is refrigerated. Never garnish any food with a flower unless you are certain the flower is edible.
- Candied violets and other blossoms are whimsical, ready-made decorations. They can be found in many gourmet shops and supermarkets. A little goes a long way; use them sparingly.
- A sprinkling of nuts is always welcome. Chop large nuts or leave them whole. Whole almonds, walnuts and hazelnuts (filberts) are especially attractive, and once they are anchored in frosting, whipped cream or caramel, they won't slip. Dip whole nuts halfway or entirely in melted chocolate; set dipped nuts on waxed paper to dry before using. Chop pistachios

and scatter them over any frosted or creamy dessert; their brilliant green color accents dark- and light-colored desserts equally well.

- Fresh berries and thin spirals or juliennes of citrus peel can echo the flavor of the dessert or add a summery note. Use whole, perfect berries that have been washed, then gently patted dry. Dip strawberries halfway into melted chocolate; let the chocolate dry before placing the fruit on the dessert.

- Chocolate is one of the most versatile decorating tools. Shavings, curls and cutouts are the perfect garnish for an added touch of chocolate flavor. For curls and shavings, press a vegetable peeler firmly against the smooth surface of a bar of room-temperature—not chilled—chocolate; pull the peeler toward you in long strokes. Curls will be less fragile if the chocolate is slightly warm. To make cutouts, melt 4 ounces of sweet baking chocolate over low heat. Spread it over the outside bottom surface of an 8 × 8-inch pan. Refrigerate until firm, then bring to room temperature. Cut the chocolate into shapes and refrigerate until you are ready to use them.

A drizzle of melted unsweetened, bittersweet or semisweet chocolate can be elegant. Try a drizzle of melted "white chocolate" (also known as vanilla-flavored candy coating, white cocoa butter coating, confectioners' coating and summer coating) over dark desserts. Always melt chocolate over very low heat. Even a few drops of water in chocolate will cause it to "tighten" rather than melt smoothly; when melting it over hot water, take care that steam doesn't condense in the chocolate.

In a pinch, 2 tablespoons unsweetened cocoa plus 1 tablespoon melted vegetable shortening or oil can be substituted for 1 ounce unsweetened chocolate.

CHOCOLATE EQUIVALENTS

6 ounces (1 package) chips	1 cup chips
1 ounce (1 square) unsweetened	1 envelope premelted chocolate
3 ounces (3 squares) semisweet	½ cup semisweet chips

- All kinds of sweets can be beautifully finished with a dollop of whipped cream, sweetened or plain. You can go a step further and pipe the cream with the help of a decorating or pastry bag for a more polished look. Stiffly beaten cream will hold a piped design well. Whipped cream that has been beaten quite stiff with a good measure of powdered sugar can be piped the same way you would pipe frosting, if you choose any but the very smallest decorating tips. When piping whipped cream, be careful not to handle the decorating bag more than necessary, and avoid squeezing it in the middle or you will squash most of the air out of it; whipped cream, less stable than frosting, gets its volume from air that is beaten in.

Baking Cakes

- Always use pans of the size called for in the recipe. Baked in too large a pan, your cake will look flat and pale. Baked in too small a pan, it will bulge over the rim of the pan, or even overflow.
- Use shiny metal pans for baking cakes. They ensure tender, golden crusts.
- Never fill a cake pan more than half full. If you have batter left over, you can use it to make cupcakes.
- Angel food and chiffon cakes are best baked with the oven rack in the lowest position. To test whether the cake is done, touch the top lightly. If no marks remain and the cracks in the top of the cake are dry, the cake is done. These cakes are usually baked in tube pans. To cool, invert them on a heatproof funnel or narrow-necked bottle; then loosen the cake by gently sliding a metal spatula or thin knife all around the inside of the pan, using short up-and-down strokes.
- Shortening-type cakes are done when the edges pull away slightly from the sides of the pan and a wooden pick inserted in the center of the cake comes out clean.

Storing Cakes

A cake warm from the oven is very moist. Don't cover it until it has cooled completely. Always store cake filled or decorated with a cream- or custard-based mixture in the refrigerator; this includes whipped cream and cream cheese toppings and fillings. Fluffy frostings don't store as well as creamy ones, but a cake decorated with fluffy frosting will keep overnight in a cake safe or placed under a large inverted bowl (slip a knife blade under the cake safe lid or the rim of the bowl so that the covering isn't airtight). A cake decorated with creamy frosting can be stored under a cake safe, a large inverted bowl, or covered loosely with aluminum foil, plastic wrap or waxed paper.

CAKE YIELDS

CAKE	SERVINGS
8-inch layer	10 to 14
9-inch layer	12 to 16
13 × 9 × 2-inch rectangle	12 to 15
8- or 9-inch square	9
10 × 4-inch tube pan	12 to 15
12-cup bundt cake pan	12 to 15

Decorating Cakes

Frosted cakes present special decorating challenges. Always start with a cake that has cooled completely. Take the time to make sure the frosting coats the sides smoothly; a thin, flexible spatula will help you spread it evenly. Then, let your imagination roam. Many of the suggestions above apply to frosted cakes. In addition, you can use a decorating comb (made of plastic or aluminum) to make waves, ridges, swirls and scallops in the frosting before it dries. Piping frosting is another alternative, one that is fun and takes only a little practice.

Shells, flowers, leaves, twists, ribbons, borders, lettering and more are at your fingertips when you pipe frosting. If you want to pipe simple lines (as for lettering) but don't have a decorating bag, you can make a piping "cone" from a simple letter envelope: Put about ⅓ cup frosting in one corner of an envelope; fold the envelope sides toward the center. Snip off just the corner to make a tip. The more the corner is snipped away, the thicker the piping will be.

Decorating bags are made of canvas, nylon, parchment paper or plastic. Most bags need a coupler, a small cone that anchors the decorating tip to the bag with the help of a ring screw. Follow the manufacturer's instructions to assemble the bag.

The consistency of the frosting is important; the smaller or more precise the design, the firmer the frosting should be. Test the consistency; too firm, and the mixture will not go through a small tip opening. Fill the bag no more than ⅔ full. Before decorating directly onto the cake, practice first. Hold the decorating bag at a 45 degree angle to the cake surface for all designs except stars, drop flowers, dots and rosettes; for these designs, the bag should be held perpendicular to the surface. Exert steady pressure on the bag.

There are literally hundreds of decorating tips. Here are some of the most popular:

- Drop flower tips: 107, 129, 190, 217, 224, 225, 1C and 2D.
- Leaf tips: 65, 67 and 352.
- Petal tips: 101, 102, 103, 104 and 127.
- Star tips: 32, 43 and 8B.
- Writing tips: 1–4 (small), 5–12 (medium) and 1A and 2A (large).

Decorating tips are versatile. In addition to leaves, the leaf tips make lovely borders. The petal tip is used to build flowers petal by petal, but it can be used to make ribbons, bows and ruffles. Star tips can make drop flowers, rosettes, shells and borders, too. Writing tips make delicate beads, dots and balls; use them to draw flower stems and vines.

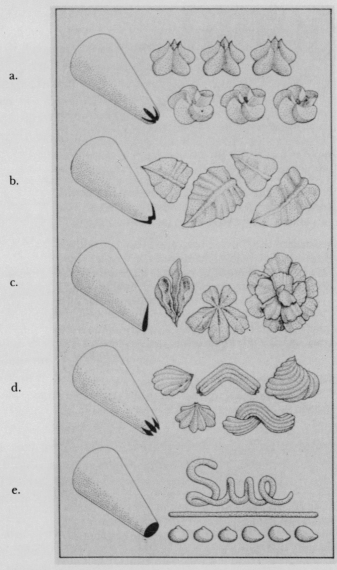

Decorating Tips and Their Use: (*a*) Drop Flower Tip, (*b*) Leaf Tip, (*c*) Petal Tip, (*d*) Star Tip, (*e*) Writing Tip

Source: General Mills, Inc.

Pie-making Tips

- A well-floured pastry cloth and stockinet-covered rolling pin help keep pastry from sticking during rolling. Rub flour into both to prevent the dough from sticking without absorbing excess flour.
- When rolling pie crust, roll from the center to the outside edge in four directions. Lift the rolling pin as it approaches the edge of the circle to ensure even thickness. Keep the pastry circular by occasionally pushing the edges in gently with your hands. Lift the pastry from time to time to check that it isn't sticking to the pastry cloth.
- Roll pastry two inches larger than the pie plate. Stretching a too-small circle of dough leads to a shrunken crust. Gently ease the crust into the pie plate, being careful not to stretch the pastry.
- Use heat-resistant glass plates for the flakiest crusts. Aluminum pans with a dull (anodized) finish are the next choice. Avoid shiny metal pans; using them results in undercooked bottom crusts.
- When baking an empty shell, prick it with a fork to keep it from puffing. You can weight it with dried beans or baking weights set in a sheet of light-weight aluminum foil; remove the foil and beans a few minutes before the pastry has finished baking.
- While pinching the top and bottom edges of a double crust together, make a rim that stands up on the edge of the pie plate; this seals the pastry and makes fluting easier.

- To prevent lumps in cream and custard fillings, stir at least half of the hot mixture into the beaten eggs first, then blend this back into the remaining hot mixture. This keeps the eggs from cooking when they are added to the hot mixture.

Pretty Crusts

Three of the easiest pastry edges can give pies a polished, professional look. For a fork edge, flatten pastry evenly with the rim of the pie plate. Press firmly around the edge with the tines of a fork. Dip the fork into flour occasionally to prevent sticking.

Another attractive but easy edge is the pinch edge. Place an index finger inside the pastry edge and the opposing thumb and index finger on the outside. Pinch the pastry into a V shape, and repeat around the edge.

A rope edge is shaped with one hand. Position the side of your thumb at an angle on the pastry edge. Pinch the pastry by pressing the knuckle of your index finger down into the pastry toward your thumb.

For a glazed crust, brush the uncooked pastry top with beaten egg or egg yolk mixed with a tablespoon of water. For a shiny crust, brush with milk. For a sugary crust, moisten the pastry lightly with water, then sprinkle with granulated sugar.

CRUMB CRUSTS FOR 9-INCH PIES

NAME	CRUMBS	MARGARINE OR BUTTER	SUGAR	TEMPERATURE AND TIME
GRAHAM CRACKER	1½ cups (about 20 squares)	⅓ cup, melted	3 tablespoons	350°, 10 minutes
COOKIE*	1½ cups	¼ cup, melted		350°, 10 minutes
GRANOLA	2 cups crushed granola	¼ cup, melted	2 tablespoons	350°, 6–8 minutes
NUT	1½ cups ground nuts	2 tablespoons, softened	3 tablespoons	400°, 6–8 minutes

*Vanilla or chocolate wafers or gingersnaps.

Mix all ingredients. Press mixture firmly against bottom and side of pie plate, 9 × 1¼ inches. Bake as directed above; cool.

Trouble Shooters and Hints

- Molded desserts sometimes do not slip easily out of their molds. Loosen the edge all around the dessert with the tip of a knife, tilting the mold as you do so to help loosen the vacuum. Dip the mold up to the rim in very warm water. Immediately take the mold out of the water, pat it dry and place the serving plate on top. Turn the mold and plate right side up. Shake gently. If the dessert doesn't slip out, dip the mold again and repeat the above steps.
- We use eggs that are graded "large." For the highest meringue, use egg whites that have stood at room temperature (but no longer than 30 minutes). Separate eggs when they are cold. Beat them in a scrupulously clean, dry bowl with clean beaters; any trace of yolk or grease will prevent them from mounting as high. Cream of tartar helps stabilize their volume.

  Beat in sugar gradually, sprinkling in each addition slowly. Continue beating until the mixture is stiff and glossy. Do not underbeat or the sugar will not dissolve properly. Rub some meringue between your fingers; if it is grainy rather than smooth, continue beating.
- Toasting enhances the flavor of many nuts. Heat the oven to 350°. Bake the nuts in an ungreased pan, stirring occasionally, until they are golden brown, 5 to 10 minutes. Watch carefully to avoid burning.

Freezing Cakes and Pies

CAKES: Plain cake freezes more successfully than frosted. Place the cooled cake in a sturdy container, cover it tightly with a layer of plastic wrap, then aluminum foil. Unfrosted cake can be frozen for 3 to 4 months. (You can freeze the cake already cut into serving pieces; these portions will thaw more quickly than the whole cake would.) When freezing a frosted cake, you can keep frosting from coming off on the wrapping. Freeze the cake uncovered for 1 hour, insert wooden picks around the top and sides of the cake, and wrap. Freeze for 2 to 3 months. Fudge and powdered sugar icings freeze especially well.

PIES: For best results, bake a pie shell before freezing. Uncooked pie shells can be frozen, but they should be put into the oven straight from the freezer, before they thaw. They last about 2 months; baked empty shells last 4 months. Meringue toppings do not freeze well, nor do cream or custard pies. Let frozen pie thaw for 1½ hours in the refrigerator.

Fast, Fresh Fruit

The freshest dessert imaginable is one of the quickest to prepare: fruit. With a light sprinkling of sugar, tossed with a few tablespoons of juice or liqueur, or *au naturel,* fruit has unique elegance. Select fully ripe fruit; it should be unblemished and have a marvelous aroma. Carefully wash and/or peel it as necessary. Taste it for sweetness. If adding sugar, refrigerate the fruit for an hour or so before serving, gently stirring the fruit occasionally.

A squeeze of fresh lime or lemon accents the natural sweetness of honeydew, cantaloupe, casaba, Persian melon and papaya.

Fresh Fruit Guide

APPLES: Choose firm apples without bruises or soft spots. The flesh of apples discolors after paring; to prevent this, sprinkle pared apples with lemon juice, or immerse it in water mixed with lemon juice. Varieties excellent for baking include Granny Smith, Greening, Pippin, Starr and Rome Beauty. Apples excellent for pies include Cortland, Rhode Island, Greening, McIntosh and Yellow Tranparent. For eating out of hand, choose Delicious, McIntosh, Jonathan and Winesap.

APRICOTS: Choose firm, golden yellow fruit that yields slightly to gentle pressure. The skin should be smooth and velvety.

AVOCADOS: Though many people think of avocados as vegetables, they are true fruits. The skins of avocados may be varying shades of green and either smooth or pebbled. The skin of a ripe avocado yields to gentle pressure. Avocados, like some other perishable fruits, are picked and shipped when they are still quite hard. They ripen best at room temperature (to encourage quick ripening, close the fruits in a paper or plastic bag). Sprinkle peeled avocado with lemon juice to keep the flesh from discoloring.

BANANAS: Choose bananas that are yellow or yellow tipped with green and unbruised spots. Ripeness is a matter of preference. The more speckled with brown the skin, the sweeter the fruit. Sprinkle peeled bananas with lemon juice to keep the flesh from discoloring.

BLACKBERRIES: Choose dark, plump, shiny berries. Ripe berries are somewhat soft— never hard. Glance over the berries and check the bottom of the container for mold.

BLUEBERRIES: Choose dark blue-purple berries. Very small berries tend to be hard and/or unripe.

CHERRIES: Sweet cherries are dark red when ripe, but ripe Queen Annes are gold touched with red. Look for plump, smooth-skinned cherries.

COCONUTS: Choose coconuts that seem heavy for their size. When you shake a coconut, you should be able to hear liquid inside. Avoid dried-out coconuts and those with mold around the eyes (the dark spots on one end).

To open a coconut, pierce the eyes with an ice pick or other suitable sharp object. Drain the coconut liquid. To break the shell, freeze the coconut for about 1 hour.

Hit the frozen coconut sharply in the middle with a hammer. The coconut flesh should be easy to separate from the shell. Coconut should be stored, tightly covered, in the refrigerator.

CRANBERRIES: Fresh cranberries are usually purchased in plastic bags. Berries should be plump, shiny and an even, deep red. Soft or wrinkled berries should be discarded.

FIGS: Figs may be a variety of shapes and colors (pale green, brownish, purple). They must be tree-ripened; ripe figs yield to gentle pressure. Overripe figs are very soft and have a sour aroma.

GOOSEBERRIES: Choose soft, ripe, light green berries. Too sour for eating raw, gooseberries are usually at least lightly cooked with sugar.

GRAPEFRUIT: Grapefruit are ripe when picked. Choose heavy, firm fruits with smooth skins. Avoid fruits with pointed ends and/or rough skin, indicating dryness.

GRAPES: Choose plump grapes that are firmly attached to the green stems. The grapes in a bunch should be of approximately the same size; grapes significantly smaller will be less ripe. Dark varieties should not be green, and green varieties should have an amber cast.

GUAVAS: Choose fruits with green or yellow skin, depending on the variety. The size may vary from small, walnut-sized fruits to fruits as large as apples.

KIWIFRUIT: These fruits are ripe when picked. Choose plump fruits with unmarked skins. Ripe kiwifruit yields slightly to gentle pressure.

KUMQUATS: Choose firm, plump fruit that has an even orange gold color.

LYCHEES: Choose lychees shaped like large strawberries with intact, evenly colored shells; avoid shriveled fruits (lychees are eaten as nuts when dried).

MANGOES: Choose slightly soft, plump fragrant fruits with red-gold, green-flecked skins. Fruits that are hard or entirely green are unripe; very soft fruits with black spots are overripe.

MELONS (SEE ALSO WATERMELON): These general rules apply to all varieties of melon except watermelon: Choose fragrant, firm, heavy melons with even color. If the stem is still attached, the fruit was picked too early; avoid soft or bruised melons.

NECTARINES: Choose plump, slightly firm fruit that is yellowish orange with a red blush; avoid bruised fruit.

ORANGES: Seedless navel oranges are best for eating, Valencia oranges for juice; oranges that seem heavy for their size are juicy. The fruit is ripe when picked, even if greenish in color.

PAPAYAS: Choose plump fruit with smooth, unblemished skin. Color indicates ripeness and ranges from green (unripe) to orangey yellow (fully ripe); avoid bruised fruit.

PEACHES: Choose plump, firm fruit that yields only slightly to gentle pressure. Ripe peaches are creamy gold, often with a pink or red blush; hard, greenish yellow peaches are unripe; avoid bruised fruit.

PEARS: Choose firm pears and allow them to fully ripen at room temperature. Ripe fruit yields to gentle pressure. Color varies with variety; avoid bruised or soft fruit.

PERSIMMONS: Choose plump, bright orange fruits. Ripe persimmons are soft; when they are even slightly firm, they are unpleasantly astringent.

PINEAPPLES: Choose fragrant, slightly firm fruit that seems heavy for its size. The leaves should be green and be easy to pull out; avoid bruised or soft fruit.

PLUMS: Choose firm—not hard—plums with smooth, evenly colored skins. Color may vary from a medium blue to purple-black. Avoid bruised or soft fruit.

POMEGRANATES: Choose a full, heavy pomegranate with smooth, unblemished skin. The larger the fruit, the larger and juicier the seeds.

QUINCES: Choose large, firm, smooth, light-yellow fruits.

RASPBERRIES: Choose plump berries of dusky, medium-to-dark red color, without stems. Glance over the berries and check the bottom of the container for mold.

RHUBARB: Choose firm, crisp stalks; if leaves are attached, they should look fresh. Color varies from light pink to ruby red. (Warning: Do not eat the leaves; they are toxic.)

STRAWBERRIES: Choose plump, bright red berries with fresh-looking green caps; avoid shriveled or moldy berries.

TANGERINES: Choose fruits with shiny, bright orange skins. The skins are naturally loose, so tangerines will not feel firm; avoid fruits with soft spots.

WATERMELONS: Choose a whole watermelon that seems heavy for its size. The rind is usually striated in color, varying from milky jade to green.

SEASONAL BUYING GUIDE

FRUIT	PEAK SEASON
Apples	September to April
Apricots	June and July
Avocados	All year
Bananas	All year
Blueberries	June to August
Cantaloupe	May to October
Cherries, sweet	June to August
Cranberries	September to February
Grapefruit	October to June
Grapes	June to January
Kiwifruit	June to March
Lemons and limes	All year
Melons, honeydew	March to November
Nectarines	June to October
Oranges	November to July
Peaches	June to October
Pears, Bartlett	July to December
D'Anjou	October to June
Pineapple	April to June
Plums	June to October
Pomegranates	September to January
Raspberries	June to August
Rhubarb	January to August
Strawberries	May to July
Tangerines	November to March
Watermelon	May to September

Desserts to Prepare in Advance

Most cakes and pies are usually prepared in advance. The desserts that follow should be prepared at least 3 hours in advance of serving.

MOUSSES AND MOLDED CREAMS

- Mango Mousse
- Orange Bavarian Cream
- Berry Pirouette
- Fudge Soufflé
- Lemon Soufflé
- Lemon Schaum Torte

PUDDINGS AND CUSTARDS

- Chocolate Pots de Crème
- Chocolate Terrine
- Almond Custard with Litchis

FROZEN DESSERTS

- Pineapple Ice
- Cranberry Ice
- Strawberry Ice Cream
- Honey–Vanilla Bean Ice Cream
- Garden Apple Ice Cream
- Frozen Rum Charlotte with Chocolate Sauce
- Hawaiian Ice Cream Dessert
- Frozen Cherry Cream
- Creamy Pumpkin Squares
- Frozen Mocha-Almond Dessert

FRUIT AND NATURALLY SWEET DESSERTS

- Sliced Oranges with Dates
- Gingered Pineapple
- Pineapple with Port
- Pears Stuffed with Dates

INDEX

V.P., Publisher: Anne M. Zeman
Project Editor: Rebecca W. Atwater
Editorial Assistant: Rachel A. Simon
Photographer: Anthony Johnson
Food Stylist: Paul Grimes
Designers: Patricia Fabricant, Frederick J. Latasa
Production Manager: Lessley Davis
Production Editor: Kimberly Ebert